the book of

job

authorized king james version

grove press
new york

with an introduction by | charles frazier

*The Pocket Canons were originally published in the U.K. in 1998 by
Canongate Books, Ltd.*
Published simultaneously in Canada
Printed in the United States of America

FIRST AMERICAN EDITION

Copyright information is on file with the Library of Congress
ISBN 0-8021-3612-5

Design by Paddy Cramsie

Grove Press
841 Broadway
New York, NY 10003

99 00 01 02   10 9 8 7 6 5 4 3 2 1

a note about pocket canons

The Authorized King James Version of the Bible, translated between 1603 and 1611, coincided with an extraordinary flowering of English literature. This version, more than any other, and possibly more than any other work in history, has had an influence in shaping the language we speak and write today. Presenting individual books from the Bible as separate volumes, as they were originally conceived, encourages the reader to approach them as literary works in their own right.

The first twelve books in this series encompass categories as diverse as history, fiction, philosophy, love poetry, and law. Each Pocket Canon also has its own introduction, specially commissioned from an impressive range of writers, which provides a personal interpretation of the text and explores its contemporary relevance.

Charles Frazier is the author of the novel Cold Mountain, *which won the National Book Award. He, his wife, and their daughter have a farm in Raleigh, North Carolina, where they raise horses.*

introduction by charles frazier

> Have pity upon me, have pity upon me,
> O ye my friends;
> for the hand of God hath touched me.   (19:21)

As a piece of writing, the great Book of Job strikes me as somewhat similar to watching people thresh grain with a herd of horses: it is all kinds of things trying to go in many different directions at once. Among these are a desperate plea for ultimate justice, an examination of how the individual relates to force and authority, an eloquent and affecting cry of despair, a great and healing song of the power of Creation, and a turgid philosophical drama patched together with a framing device that apparently includes leftover bits of a considerably more ancient Mesopotamian happy-ever-after folktale. Most strikingly, it tells what a fearful and sorrowful thing it is to fall into the hands of a torn and discordant God.

Mark Twain, in his late bitter years, wrote frequently about the Bible. He called the Old Testament's account of God's doings "perhaps the most damnatory biography that exists in print anywhere." Twain catalogs the offenses: "He was an unfair God; he was a God of unsound judgment; he was a God of failures and miscalculations; he was given to odd ideas and fantastic devices."

To be sure, the Book of Job is filled with such behavior. The plot, frail as it is, hinges on a troubling bet between God and Satan—depicted not as real enemies but as affable adversaries. Satan is rather less the Prince of Darkness here than a folk-loric trickster figure, slyly but pointedly challenging power and authority. The wager, a test of Job's faith, requires the murder of all Job's ten children and countless servants, the theft and arson of all his vast holdings. This is a measure of destructiveness that even God—at the very least an accessory to these crimes—later calls "without cause."

God initiates the action, dangling Job in Satan's face, saying, "Hast thou considered my servant Job." He calls Job "perfect," holds him out as an example of "an upright man, one that feareth God." Satan very reasonably takes the implied challenge, arguing that the prosperous Job has little reason for fear, since he has always been protected by God: "But put forth thine hand now, and touch all that he hath, and he will curse thee to thy face," Satan says.

God—apparently forgetting his own omniscience in the heat of the moment—falls for this trap and gives Satan almost free rein to test his theory, restraining him in but one regard: "Only upon himself [Job] put not forth thine hand." So Satan pours down tornadic winds, marauding Sabeans and Chaldeans, and the fire of God from Heaven. Job responds much as God expects: he tears his clothes, shaves his head, and falls on the ground to pray, saying, among other things:

the Lord gave, and the Lord hath taken away;
blessed be the name of the Lord.   (1:21)

Kierkegaard, in his Discourse on Job, makes much of that pair of lines, and he appears to have lost interest at this point, choosing to see Job as a story of unquestioning faith in the face of adversity. Satan, on the other hand, is not yet ready to call the game. He suggests that one's property is one thing, "But put forth thine hand now, and touch his bone and his flesh, and he will curse thee to thy face." With God's blessing Satan then smites Job with boils from crown to sole, leaving him sitting in an ash heap scraping his sores with a potsherd. Job's wife's best advice at this most recent downturn in fortune is that he should "curse God, and die." Job, though, insists on some accounting. What did he do to call down such weight of calamity? Not a thing that he can figure. As stand-in for mankind under constant attack—both physical and spiritual—until woe overbrims our frail vessels, Job demands an explanation for his fate, some justice, an assurance of cosmic fairness. Lacking that, he demands at the very least a chance to yowl his fear and despair at a God that by all the evidence of his actions holds man in contempt and the strictures of justice that bind civilized cultures in weak regard.

For the arrows of the Almighty are within me,
the poison whereof drinketh up my spirit:
the terrors of God do set themselves
in array against me.   (6:4)

At Enfield, Connecticut, in 1741, Jonathan Edwards delivered the most famous of American sermons, "Sinners in the Hands of an Angry God." Edwards's violent, unknowable God, like the one in the Book of Job, expresses much of His power through boundless and easily provoked rage. This is the way Edwards recommends we consider such a Deity:

> How awful are those words, Isaiah 63:3, which are the words of the great God: "I will tread them in mine anger, and trample them in my fury; and their blood shall be sprinkled upon my garments, and I will stain all my raiment." It is perhaps impossible to conceive of words that carry in them greater manifestations of these three things, viz., contempt, and hatred, and fierceness of indignation. If you cry to God to pity you, He will be so far from pitying you in your doleful case, or showing you the least regard or favor, that instead of that He will only tread you under foot; and though He will know that you cannot bear the weight of omnipotence treading upon you, He will not regard that, but He will crush you under His feet without mercy; He will crush out your blood and make it fly, and it shall be sprinkled on His garments, so as to stain all His raiment. He will not only hate you, but He will have you in the utmost contempt; no place shall be thought fit for you but under his feet, to be trodden down as mire in the streets.

In the city and suburban churches of the current version of America, God is really not much that way at all anymore. On the rare occasions I attend such churches, I am struck with the overriding conviction of pastor and congregation that to the extent God is angry at anyone, it is certainly not with people remotely like you and me. God's dark moods have lifted. He is love, and our flaws are really quite understandable and totally forgivable. So minor indeed that, honestly, personal change—at least of any radical or inconvenient kind—is not in order, not the least bit called for.

It is only when I am driving in the rural bits of the country—the regions—that I find any remnant of the old mad God of Edwards and Job, and that confined to the extremes of the AM band where vestigial spittle-spewing preachers rant the breathless and urgent message that God might very well despise us all, and with good cause. It is easy to ridicule such men, to find them humorous or, worse, quaint. But it may be a dangerous proposition to dismiss their views out of hand. Look about you; go to and fro in the world, walk up and down in it like Satan in the Book of Job; make a fair report and then try to present a convincing argument against them.

When I say, My bed shall comfort me,
my couch shall ease my complaint;
Then thou scarest me with dreams,
and terrifiest me through visions;
So that my soul chooseth strangling,
and death rather than my life.   (7:13-15)

In my line of work it is often incumbent upon me to read the great spiritual texts of our many people. I am fondest of the Buddhist writings, and also those of various shamans and visionaries and anchorites and desert fathers. All useful in their own ways. I have not, however, read the Book of Job since I was perhaps twelve, when I was, for a brief time, Methodist. Each month I took from a stand in the church foyer a copy of *The Upper Room,* a booklet of suggested daily Bible readings with suggested interpretations. The cover of it was always an artistic rendering of a biblical event, done in rich saturated colors like Caravaggio or Dell Comics. My Bible had a black leather zippered cover with my name stamped in gold letters, and for a bookmark I used a cross twisted from a palm frond. It was the height of the Cold War, and I read the Bible with a certain superstitious consistency every night before turning out the light and tuning in to WLAC's fifty thousand clear watts through the earphone of a gray plastic Zenith transistor radio.

I had trouble sleeping. We lived in a cup of Appalachian valley that lay as the crow flies only a short way from Oak Ridge, a place all my teachers assured me was a first target for Soviet nuclear attack. Some of my friends had bomb shelters buried underneath their houses. You reached them through twisting tunnels, as if visiting the tombs of pharaohs. Inside were canned goods, jugs of water, reading matter. All the things you'd need when you got to the other side. We did not have a shelter.

Sometimes as I lay awake listening to Stax and Chess R&B—John R and Daddy Gene emphatically naming the tunes and reading mail-order offers for Ernie's Record Mart and a thousand baby chicks—I was convinced that this night was the night it all would fall. The siren down at the town fire station would sound, and then before I even had time to get out of bed, the whole broad sky out the window would flash up bright as the flame at the tip of a welder's torch toward which one dare not look.

My bedroom window opened out onto our neighbor's house. It was a log cabin with pale plaster chinking between the dark logs. It sat under a big black walnut tree, and the man that lived alone in it was a sweet old drunk who woke every morning at four no matter what shape he was in or what hour the sun rose. If we locked our keys in our house he would come over with a hammer and a screwdriver and make a single delicate tap and the door would spring open. When, long before dawn, he turned on his lights, it seemed to me that the night watch had changed and I could go to sleep. Old Doug was awake behind his yellow windows, and not much bad could happen.

> Therefore I will not refrain my mouth;
> I will speak in the anguish of my spirit;
> I will complain in the bitterness of my soul.   (7:11)

So there sits Job, on the wrong side of God, scraping his boils with a sherd, wondering what he did wrong. And saddled with such a wife. Then three old friends——Bildad the Shuhite, Zophar the Naamathite, and Eliphaz the Temanite——show up to sit with him. They do not, however, commiserate with him; they argue at great length that despite the severity and apparent injustice of his afflictions, he must have had it coming. They're not sure why, but there has to be a reason. Undeserved suffering cannot be. William Blake, in plate X of his *Illustrations of the Book of Job*, shows these men kneeling, their staring faces close together in expressions of self-righteous

charles frazier   xiii condemnation, all bearing a great family resemblance to demons. They all point at weeping Job with the fingers of their hands held in creepy, incantatory gestures.

In Blake's reading of Job, despair seems to come—if not wholly, at least significantly—from isolation, a devastating inturning that finds visual expression in several ways. One is a lonely set-apartness in the relation of Job to other human figures in the plates; they turn from him, space themselves away from him, hide their faces from him. They draw away; he pulls into himself. Or the other way around. When they do look at him, they mock and scorn and condemn. Most affectingly, Job's isolation is evident in the odd and troubling resemblances of God, Satan, and Job—as if Blake were suggesting that Job has fallen so far in upon himself that he has created a God and a Devil in his own image.

It is at this point in the narrative that Job—utterly ruined, all his vast holdings and the people he presumably loved yanked from him—begins speaking powerful poems cursing his personal existence. "Why me, Lord" is a good question, and one we've all cast out at one time or another to an unresponsive universe. But Job fashions the simple query into some of the greatest and most terse expressions of despair and soul weariness we have. Job's laments are as blunt and stripped in their pain as Delta blues. I'd like to think there's influence there, to imagine Charlie Patton sitting down with a huge limp Bible flapped open on his lap to chapter 3 of Job and then switching to his guitar and making up "When Your Way Gets Dark" or "Down the Dirt Road." I'll just point out, rather at random, some personal high points of Job's blues: "My face is foul with weeping, and on my eyelids is the shadow of death" (16:16); "My days are swifter than a weaver's shuttle, and are spent without hope" (7:6); "My soul is weary of my life" (10:1); "My days are past, my purposes are broken off, even the thoughts of my heart" (17:11); "For now shall I sleep in the dust; and thou shalt seek me in the morning, but I shall not be" (7:21).

It is some reimbursement, at least, with everything you have taken from you, everything you desire denied you, everything you fear come to pass, to have language of such force and simplicity at your command as both weapon and balm.

Hast thou perceived the breadth of the earth?
Declare if thou knowest it all.   (38:18)

One of the central questions the Book of Job asks is: How might man and Deity communicate in order to settle the issues Job raises? Job offers logic as a path. "Surely I would speak to the Almighty, and I would desire to reason with God," he says (13:3). It is tempting to view God's entrance in a whirlwind and his subsequent boastful listing of his creative accomplishments, his power and authority as dodging the question, a victory of force over reason, of fear over all else. The Almighty supports such a reading when He asks, "Hast thou an arm like God? Or canst thou thunder with a voice like him?" (40:9).

But his long speech also offers hope for an alternative reading, one that proposes quite a different channel of communication than the one Job recommends. What God holds out for consideration is Creation, all that is the world, its bigness and smallness, its infinite detail, its differing statements of motif and theme, their complex variations and repetitions, beauty and terror intermixed. It is a construct so finely made that even its wild and violent and enormous elements— Leviathan is an example God offers with particular pleasure— contain in their details the smallest and most delicate elements, for the eyes of the monster are "like the eyelids of the morning" (41:18). God is also rightfully pleased with the concept and execution of water in its various forms, rain and dew and ice and frost. His pride is the understandable pride of the artist who has succeeded in creating a whole world. The details of horse anatomy, he feels, worked out particularly well: "The glory of his nostrils is terrible" (39:20).

Blake seems to have liked this line too, for in plate XIV— his illustration of this bit of the text—one of the details of Creation he chooses to include are four horses, nostrils flaring. Blake's God stares out from this frame, just missing eye contact with the viewer, an oddly stricken expression on His face, but His arms are stretched out to encompass ranks of jubilant angels, stars, beasts and humans, mountains and rivers, birds and plants and creeping things. Look at it all, God seems to be saying. Don't trouble me with reason; what you need to know is there in the art and the mystery and ultimate unknowableness of my elegant design. Love it and fear it. Submit to it.

For the thing which I greatly feared
is come upon me, and that
which I was afraid of is come unto me.   (3:25)

A number of years ago I read the account of Black Elk, an old Sioux visionary and a friend of Crazy Horse. He lived to see catastrophes to his people at least the like of Job's. They lost as close to everything as you can and not just be extinct. He lived on past his particular apocalypse, to be another exile in the twentieth century. In telling his story, he dwells in great detail on a time in his earlier life when he had become consumed with fear, "afraid of being afraid." He then had a powerful vision that featured the four quarters of the earth, the weathers of the sky, animals and man. In other words, all of Creation. The great lesson of this all-encompassing vision was the conviction that we should not fear the universe. I remember writing the line down in a lost notebook along with a poem by Stephen Dunn and some lines from a Thomas McGuane novel expressing what struck me as somewhat the same ideas.

Not fearing the universe is a useful and comforting attitude if you can sustain it. And with varying degrees of success, I've tried to do it many times. Once I was lost in the Bolivian cloud forest, the damp brow of mountain between the Andes and the Amazon. I had walked down from a barren eighteen-thousand-foot pass, and gradually my map and the land came more and more to disresemble one another. And then fairly suddenly the trail was gone. My one companion waited by a river for me to scout a route.

I walked a mile or so, contouring around a heavily treed hillside and over a ridge, and then I came to a high cliff. Stretched out far beneath my feet was the Amazon basin. I could see for what must have been a hundred miles before the jungle faded into haze. There was not a road or clearing or feather of smoke, just unmarked green treetops. It was a sensation similar to lying on your back in a Cherry County,

Nebraska, field and looking up into the moonless night sky. So to say, the legendary indifference of nature to man's individual existence was much in evidence. I sat on a rock for a long time looking out, and one of the word-strings I remember crossing my mind was, Do not fear the universe. I remember that it helped. And that is about all that you can ask of words.

I thought them again after two days of bushwhacking, when in the dark I stumbled through a banana grove and cutters came out from their camp and stood with machetes in their hands, the thick blades backlit in the glare of pressurized gas lanterns. As it turned out, the men were as scared of me and my thrashing as I was of them. They had warm beer in liter bottles, and they showed me where to camp. I slept by a black river and the night was so quiet I could hear the rocks in the riverbed moving against each other in the current.

It is easy enough when the universe behaves in such a benign way not to fear it. But the Book of Job and its God of the whirlwind are of a different turn of mind. They say—also usefully—"Yes, sometimes do."

the book of job

There was a man in the land of Uz, whose name was Job; and that man was perfect and upright, and one that feared God, and eschewed evil. ²And there were born unto him seven sons and three daughters. ³His substance also was seven thousand sheep, and three thousand camels, and five hundred yoke of oxen, and five hundred she asses, and a very great household; so that this man was the greatest of all the men of the east. ⁴And his sons went and feasted in their houses, every one his day; and sent and called for their three sisters to eat and to drink with them. ⁵And it was so, when the days of their feasting were gone about, that Job sent and sanctified them, and rose up early in the morning, and offered burnt offerings according to the number of them all: for Job said, 'It may be that my sons have sinned, and cursed God in their hearts.' Thus did Job continually.

⁶Now there was a day when the sons of God came to present themselves before the Lord, and Satan came also among them. ⁷And the Lord said unto Satan, 'Whence comest thou?' Then Satan answered the Lord, and said, 'From going to and fro in the earth, and from walking up and down in it.' ⁸And the Lord said unto Satan, 'Hast thou considered my servant Job, that there is none like him in the earth, a perfect

and an upright man, one that feareth God, and escheweth evil?' ⁹ Then Satan answered the Lord, and said, 'Doth Job fear God for nought? ¹⁰ Hast not thou made an hedge about him, and about his house, and about all that he hath on every side? Thou hast blessed the work of his hands, and his substance is increased in the land. ¹¹ But put forth thine hand now, and touch all that he hath, and he will curse thee to thy face.' ¹²And the Lord said unto Satan, 'Behold, all that he hath is in thy power; only upon himself put not forth thine hand.' So Satan went forth from the presence of the Lord.

¹³And there was a day when his sons and his daughters were eating and drinking wine in their eldest brother's house, ¹⁴ and there came a messenger unto Job, and said, 'The oxen were plowing, and the asses feeding beside them; ¹⁵ and the Sabeans fell upon them, and took them away; yea, they have slain the servants with the edge of the sword; and I only am escaped alone to tell thee.' ¹⁶ While he was yet speaking, there came also another, and said, 'The fire of God is fallen from heaven, and hath burned up the sheep, and the servants, and consumed them; and I only am escaped alone to tell thee.' ¹⁷ While he was yet speaking, there came also another, and said, 'The Chaldeans made out three bands, and fell upon the camels, and have carried them away, yea, and slain the servants with the edge of the sword; and I only am escaped alone to tell thee.' ¹⁸ While he was yet speaking, there came also another, and said, 'Thy sons and thy daughters were eating and drinking wine in their eldest brother's house; ¹⁹ and, behold, there came a great wind from the wilderness, and

smote the four corners of the house, and it fell upon the young men, and they are dead; and I only am escaped alone to tell thee.' ²⁰ Then Job arose, and rent his mantle, and shaved his head, and fell down upon the ground, and worshipped, ²¹ and said,

> 'Naked came I out of my mother's womb,
> and naked shall I return thither:
> the Lord gave, and the Lord hath taken away;
> blessed be the name of the Lord.'

²² In all this Job sinned not, nor charged God foolishly.

2 Again there was a day when the sons of God came to present themselves before the Lord, and Satan came also among them to present himself before the Lord. ²And the Lord said unto Satan, 'From whence comest thou?' And Satan answered the Lord, and said, 'From going to and fro in the earth, and from walking up and down in it.' ³And the Lord said unto Satan, 'Hast thou considered my servant Job, that there is none like him in the earth, a perfect and an upright man, one that feareth God, and escheweth evil? And still he holdeth fast his integrity, although thou movedst me against him, to destroy him without cause.' ⁴And Satan answered the Lord, and said, 'Skin for skin, yea, all that a man hath will he give for his life. ⁵But put forth thine hand now, and touch his bone and his flesh, and he will curse thee to thy face.' ⁶And the Lord said unto Satan, 'Behold, he is in thine hand; but save his life.'

⁷So went Satan forth from the presence of the Lord, and smote Job with sore boils from the sole of his foot unto his crown. ⁸And he took him a potsherd to scrape himself withal; and he sat down among the ashes.

⁹Then said his wife unto him, 'Dost thou still retain thine integrity? Curse God, and die.' ¹⁰But he said unto her, 'Thou speakest as one of the foolish women speaketh. What? Shall we receive good at the hand of God, and shall we not receive evil?' In all this did not Job sin with his lips.

¹¹Now when Job's three friends heard of all this evil that was come upon him, they came every one from his own place: Eliphaz the Temanite, and Bildad the Shuhite, and Zophar the Naamathite; for they had made an appointment together to come to mourn with him and to comfort him. ¹²And when they lifted up their eyes afar off, and knew him not, they lifted up their voice, and wept; and they rent every one his mantle, and sprinkled dust upon their heads toward heaven. ¹³So they sat down with him upon the ground seven days and seven nights, and none spake a word unto him: for they saw that his grief was very great.

3 After this opened Job his mouth, and cursed his day. ²And Job spake, and said,

> ³'Let the day perish wherein I was born,
>   and the night in which it was said,
>   "There is a man child conceived."
> ⁴Let that day be darkness;

let not God regard it from above,

    neither let the light shine upon it.

⁵ Let darkness and the shadow of death stain it;

    let a cloud dwell upon it;

        let the blackness of the day terrify it.

⁶As for that night, let darkness seize upon it;

    let it not be joined unto the days of the year;

        let it not come into the number of the months.

⁷ Lo, let that night be solitary,

    let no joyful voice come therein.

⁸ Let them curse it that curse the day,

    who are ready to raise up their mourning.

⁹ Let the stars of the twilight thereof be dark;

    let it look for light, but have none;

        neither let it see the dawning of the day:

¹⁰ because it shut not up the doors of my mother's

    womb, nor hid sorrow from mine eyes.

¹¹ Why died I not from the womb?

    why did I not give up the ghost

        when I came out of the belly?

¹² Why did the knees prevent me?

    Or why the breasts that I should suck?

¹³ For now should I have lain still and been quiet,

    I should have slept: then had I been at rest,

¹⁴ with kings and counsellors of the earth,

    which built desolate places for themselves;

¹⁵ or with princes that had gold,

    who filled their houses with silver:

¹⁶ or as an hidden untimely birth I had not been;
   as infants which never saw light.
¹⁷ There the wicked cease from troubling;
   and there the weary be at rest.
¹⁸ There the prisoners rest together;
   they hear not the voice of the oppressor.
¹⁹ The small and great are there;
   and the servant is free from his master.
²⁰ Wherefore is light given to him that is in misery,
   and life unto the bitter in soul;
²¹ which long for death, but it cometh not,
   and dig for it more than for hid treasures;
²² which rejoice exceedingly, and are glad,
   when they can find the grave?
²³ Why is light given to a man whose way is hid,
   and whom God hath hedged in?
²⁴ For my sighing cometh before I eat,
   and my roarings are poured out like the waters.
²⁵ For the thing which I greatly feared
   is come upon me, and that
      which I was afraid of is come unto me.
²⁶ I was not in safety, neither had I rest,
   neither was I quiet; yet trouble came.'

4 Then Eliphaz the Temanite answered and said, ² 'If we assay to commune with thee, wilt thou be grieved? But who can withhold himself from speaking? ³ Behold, thou hast instructed many, and thou hast strengthened the weak hands.

⁴ Thy words have upholden him that was falling, and thou hast strengthened the feeble knees. ⁵ But now it is come upon thee, and thou faintest; it toucheth thee, and thou art troubled. ⁶ Is not this thy fear, thy confidence, thy hope, and the uprightness of thy ways? ⁷ Remember, I pray thee, who ever perished, being innocent? Or where were the righteous cut off? ⁸ Even as I have seen, they that plow iniquity, and sow wickedness, reap the same. ⁹ By the blast of God they perish, and by the breath of his nostrils are they consumed. ¹⁰ The roaring of the lion, and the voice of the fierce lion, and the teeth of the young lions, are broken. ¹¹ The old lion perisheth for lack of prey, and the stout lion's whelps are scattered abroad. ¹² Now a thing was secretly brought to me, and mine ear received a little thereof. ¹³ In thoughts from the visions of the night, when deep sleep falleth on men, ¹⁴ fear came upon me, and trembling, which made all my bones to shake. ¹⁵ Then a spirit passed before my face; the hair of my flesh stood up. ¹⁶ It stood still, but I could not discern the form thereof: an image was before mine eyes, there was silence, and I heard a voice, saying, ¹⁷ "Shall mortal man be more just than God? Shall a man be more pure than his maker? ¹⁸ Behold, he put no trust in his servants; and his angels he charged with folly; ¹⁹ how much less in them that dwell in houses of clay, whose foundation is in the dust, which are crushed before the moth? ²⁰ They are destroyed from morning to evening; they perish for ever without any regarding it. ²¹ Doth not their excellency which is in them go away? They die, even without wisdom.'"

5 'Call now, if there be any that will answer thee; and to which of the saints wilt thou turn? ² For wrath killeth the foolish man, and envy slayeth the silly one. ³ I have seen the foolish taking root; but suddenly I cursed his habitation. ⁴ His children are far from safety, and they are crushed in the gate, neither is there any to deliver them. ⁵ Whose harvest the hungry eateth up, and taketh it even out of the thorns, and the robber swalloweth up their substance. ⁶ Although affliction cometh not forth of the dust, neither doth trouble spring out of the ground; ⁷ yet man is born unto trouble, as the sparks fly upward. ⁸ I would seek unto God, and unto God would I commit my cause: ⁹ which doeth great things and unsearchable, marvellous things without number; ¹⁰ who giveth rain upon the earth, and sendeth waters upon the fields; ¹¹ to set up on high those that be low, that those which mourn may be exalted to safety. ¹² He disappointeth the devices of the crafty, so that their hands cannot perform their enterprise. ¹³ He taketh the wise in their own craftiness; and the counsel of the forward is carried headlong. ¹⁴ They meet with darkness in the daytime, and grope in the noonday as in the night. ¹⁵ But he saveth the poor from the sword, from their mouth, and from the hand of the mighty. ¹⁶ So the poor hath hope, and iniquity stoppeth her mouth. ¹⁷ Behold, happy is the man whom God correcteth; therefore despise not thou the chastening of the Almighty: ¹⁸ for he maketh sore, and bindeth up; he woundeth, and his hands make whole. ¹⁹ He shall deliver thee in six troubles; yea, in seven there shall no evil touch thee. ²⁰ In famine he shall redeem thee from death;

and in war from the power of the sword. ²¹ Thou shalt be hid from the scourge of the tongue; neither shalt thou be afraid of destruction when it cometh. ²² At destruction and famine thou shalt laugh; neither shalt thou be afraid of the beasts of the earth. ²³ For thou shalt be in league with the stones of the field; and the beasts of the field shall be at peace with thee. ²⁴ And thou shalt know that thy tabernacle shall be in peace; and thou shalt visit thy habitation, and shalt not sin. ²⁵ Thou shalt know also that thy seed shall be great, and thine offspring as the grass of the earth. ²⁶ Thou shalt come to thy grave in a full age, like as a shock of corn cometh in his season. ²⁷ Lo this, we have searched it, so it is; hear it, and know thou it for thy good.'

6 But Job answered and said,

²'Oh that my grief were throughly weighed,
   and my calamity laid in the balances together!
³ For now it would be heavier
   than the sand of the sea;
      therefore my words are swallowed up.
⁴ For the arrows of the Almighty are within me,
   the poison whereof drinketh up my spirit:
      the terrors of God do set themselves
      in array against me.
⁵ Doth the wild ass bray when he hath grass?
   Or loweth the ox over his fodder?
⁶ Can that which is unsavoury be eaten without salt?

Or is there any taste in the white of an egg?
⁷ The things that my soul refused to touch
   are as my sorrowful meat.
⁸ Oh that I might have my request; and that
   God would grant me the thing that I long for!
⁹ Even that it would please God to destroy me;
   that he would let loose his hand, and cut me off!
¹⁰ Then should I yet have comfort;
   yea, I would harden myself in sorrow:
      let him not spare; for I have not concealed
      the words of the Holy One.
¹¹ What is my strength, that I should hope?
   And what is mine end,
      that I should prolong my life?
¹² Is my strength the strength of stones?
   Or is my flesh of brass?
¹³ Is not my help in me?
   And is wisdom driven quite from me?
¹⁴ To him that is afflicted pity
   should be shewed from his friend;
      but he forsaketh the fear of the Almighty.
¹⁵ My brethren have dealt deceitfully as a brook,
   and as the stream of brooks they pass away;
¹⁶ which are blackish by reason of the ice,
   and wherein the snow is hid.
¹⁷ What time they wax warm, they vanish;
   when it is hot,
      they are consumed out of their place.

¹⁸ The paths of their way are turned aside;
    they go to nothing, and perish.
¹⁹ The troops of Tema looked,
    the companies of Sheba waited for them.
²⁰ They were confounded because they had hoped;
    they came thither, and were ashamed.
²¹ For now ye are nothing;
    ye see my casting down, and are afraid.
²² Did I say, "Bring unto me?"
    or, "Give a reward for me of your substance?"
²³ or, "Deliver me from the enemy's hand?"
    or, "Redeem me from the hand of the mighty?"
²⁴ Teach me, and I will hold my tongue;
    and cause me to understand
        wherein I have erred.
²⁵ How forcible are right words!
    But what doth your arguing reprove?
²⁶ Do ye imagine to reprove words,
    and the speeches of one that is desperate,
        which are as wind?
²⁷ Yea, ye overwhelm the fatherless,
    and ye dig a pit for your friend.
²⁸ Now therefore be content, look upon me;
    for it is evident unto you if I lie.
²⁹ Return, I pray you, let it not be iniquity;
    yea, return again, my righteousness is in it.
³⁰ Is there iniquity in my tongue?
    Cannot my taste discern perverse things?'

7

'Is there not an appointed time to man upon earth?
　　Are not his days also like the days of an hireling?
²As a servant earnestly desireth the shadow, and as
　　an hireling looketh for the reward of his work,
³ so am I made to possess months of vanity,
　　and wearisome nights are appointed to me.
⁴ When I lie down, I say,
　　"When shall I arise, and the night be gone?"
　　　　and I am full of tossings to and fro
　　unto the dawning of the day.
⁵ My flesh is clothed with worms and clods of dust;
　　my skin is broken, and become loathsome.
⁶ My days are swifter than a weaver's shuttle,
　　and are spent without hope.
⁷ O remember that my life is wind:
　　mine eye shall no more see good.
⁸ The eye of him that hath seen me
　　shall see me no more:
　　　　thine eyes are upon me, and I am not.
⁹ As the cloud is consumed and vanisheth away,
　　so he that goeth down to the grave
　　　　shall come up no more.
¹⁰ He shall return no more to his house,
　　neither shall his place know him any more.
¹¹ Therefore I will not refrain my mouth;
　　I will speak in the anguish of my spirit;
　　　　I will complain in the bitterness of my soul.

¹²Am I a sea, or a whale,
that thou settest a watch over me?
¹³ When I say, "My bed shall comfort me,
my couch shall ease my complaint";
¹⁴ then thou scarest me with dreams,
and terrifiest me through visions;
¹⁵ so that my soul chooseth strangling,
and death rather than my life.
¹⁶ I loathe it; I would not live alway.
Let me alone; for my days are vanity.
¹⁷ What is man, that thou shouldest magnify him?
And that thou shouldest
set thine heart upon him?
¹⁸And that thou shouldest visit him every morning,
and try him every moment?
¹⁹ How long wilt thou not depart from me,
nor let me alone till I swallow down my spittle?
²⁰ I have sinned; what shall I do unto thee,
O thou preserver of men?
Why hast thou set me as a mark against thee,
so that I am a burden to myself?
²¹And why dost thou not pardon my transgression,
and take away mine iniquity?
For now shall I sleep in the dust;
and thou shalt seek me in the morning,
but I shall not be.'

8 Then answered Bildad the Shuhite, and said, [2] 'How long wilt thou speak these things? And how long shall the words of thy mouth be like a strong wind? [3] Doth God pervert judgement? Or doth the Almighty pervert justice? [4] If thy children have sinned against him, and he have cast them away for their transgression; [5] if thou wouldest seek unto God betimes, and make thy supplication to the Almighty; [6] if thou wert pure and upright; surely now he would awake for thee, and make the habitation of thy righteousness prosperous. [7] Though thy beginning was small, yet thy latter end should greatly increase. [8] For enquire, I pray thee, of the former age, and prepare thyself to the search of their fathers [9] (for we are but of yesterday, and know nothing, because our days upon earth are a shadow). [10] Shall not they teach thee, and tell thee, and utter words out of their heart? [11] Can the rush grow up without mire? Can the flag grow without water? [12] Whilst it is yet in his greenness, and not cut down, it withereth before any other herb. [13] So are the paths of all that forget God, and the hypocrite's hope shall perish; [14] whose hope shall be cut off, and whose trust shall be a spider's web. [15] He shall lean upon his house, but it shall not stand; he shall hold it fast, but it shall not endure. [16] He is green before the sun, and his branch shooteth forth in his garden. [17] His roots are wrapped about the heap, and seeth the place of stones. [18] If he destroy him from his place, then it shall deny him, saying, I have not seen thee. [19] Behold, this is the joy of his way, and out of the earth shall others grow. [20] Behold, God will not cast away a perfect man, neither will he help the evil doers; [21] till he fill

thy mouth with laughing, and thy lips with rejoicing. ²² They
that hate thee shall be clothed with shame; and the dwelling
place of the wicked shall come to nought.'

9 Then Job answered and said,

²'I know it is so of a truth;
but how should man be just with God?
³ If he will contend with him,
he cannot answer him one of a thousand.
⁴ He is wise in heart, and mighty in strength:
who hath hardened himself against him,
and hath prospered?
⁵ Which removeth the mountains, and they know not;
which overturneth them in his anger.
⁶ Which shaketh the earth out of her place,
and the pillars thereof tremble.
⁷ Which commandeth the sun, and it riseth not;
and sealeth up the stars.
⁸ Which alone spreadeth out the heavens,
and treadeth upon the waves of the sea.
⁹ Which maketh Arcturus, Orion, and Pleiades,
and the chambers of the south.
¹⁰ Which doeth great things past finding out;
yea, and wonders without number.
¹¹ Lo, he goeth by me, and I see him not;
he passeth on also, but I perceive him not.
¹² Behold, he taketh away, who can hinder him?

Who will say unto him, "What doest thou?"

¹³ If God will not withdraw his anger,
the proud helpers do stoop under him.

¹⁴ How much less shall I answer him,
and choose out my words to reason with him?

¹⁵ Whom, though I were righteous,
yet would I not answer,
but I would make supplication to my judge.

¹⁶ If I had called, and he had answered me;
yet would I not believe that he had
hearkened unto my voice.

¹⁷ For he breaketh me with a tempest,
and multiplieth my wounds without cause.

¹⁸ He will not suffer me to take my breath,
but filleth me with bitterness.

¹⁹ If I speak of strength, lo, he is strong; and,
if of judgment, who shall set me a time to plead?

²⁰ If I justify myself, mine own mouth shall
condemn me; if I say I am perfect,
it shall also prove me perverse.

²¹ Though I were perfect,
yet would I not know my soul:
I would despise my life.

²² This is one thing, therefore I said it,
He destroyeth the perfect and the wicked.

²³ If the scourge slay suddenly,
he will laugh at the trial of the innocent.

²⁴ The earth is given into the hand of the wicked;
    he covereth the faces of the judges thereof;
        if not, where and who is he?
²⁵ Now my days are swifter than a post:
    they flee away, they see no good.
²⁶ They are passed away as the swift ships;
    as the eagle that hasteth to the prey.
²⁷ If I say, "I will forget my complaint,
    I will leave off my heaviness,
        and comfort myself,"
²⁸ I am afraid of all my sorrows,
    I know that thou wilt not hold me innocent.
²⁹ If I be wicked, why then labour I in vain?
³⁰ If I wash myself with snow water,
    and make my hands never so clean;
³¹ yet shalt thou plunge me in the ditch,
    and mine own clothes shall abhor me.
³² For he is not a man, as I am,
    that I should answer him,
        and we should come together in judgment.
³³ Neither is there any daysman betwixt us,
    that might lay his hand upon us both.
³⁴ Let him take his rod away from me,
    and let not his fear terrify me;
³⁵ then would I speak, and not fear him;
    but it is not so with me.'

10 'My soul is weary of my life;
　　　I will leave my complaint upon myself;
　　　　　I will speak in the bitterness of my soul.
² I will say unto God, "Do not condemn me;
　　　shew me wherefore thou contendest with me.
³ Is it good unto thee that thou shouldest oppress,
　　　that thou shouldest despise the work of thine hands,
　　　　　and shine upon the counsel of the wicked?
⁴ Hast thou eyes of flesh? Or seest thou as man seeth?
⁵ Are thy days as the days of man?
　　　Are thy years as man's days,
⁶ that thou enquirest after mine iniquity,
　　　and searchest after my sin?
⁷ Thou knowest that I am not wicked; and
　　　there is none that can deliver out of thine hand.
⁸ Thine hands have made me
　　　and fashioned me together round about;
　　　　　yet thou dost destroy me.
⁹ Remember, I beseech thee,
　　　that thou hast made me as the clay;
　　　　　and wilt thou bring me into dust again?
¹⁰ Hast thou not poured me out as milk,
　　　and curdled me like cheese?
¹¹ Thou hast clothed me with skin and flesh,
　　　and hast fenced me with bones and sinews.
¹² Thou hast granted me life and favour,
　　　and thy visitation hath preserved my spirit.
¹³ And these things hast thou hid in thine heart;

I know that this is with thee.
¹⁴ If I sin, then thou markest me,
and thou wilt not acquit me from mine iniquity.
¹⁵ If I be wicked, woe unto me;
and if I be righteous, yet will I not lift up my head.
I am full of confusion;
therefore see thou mine affliction,
¹⁶ for it increaseth.
Thou huntest me as a fierce lion;
and again thou shewest thyself
marvellous upon me.
¹⁷ Thou renewest thy witnesses against me,
and increasest thine indignation upon me;
changes and war are against me.
¹⁸ "Wherefore then hast thou brought me forth
out of the womb?
Oh that I had given up the ghost,
and no eye had seen me!
¹⁹ I should have been as though I had not been;
I should have been carried
from the womb to the grave.
²⁰ Are not my days few?
Cease then, and let me alone,
that I may take comfort a little,
²¹ before I go whence I shall not return,
even to the land of darkness
and the shadow of death;
²² a land of darkness, as darkness itself;

and of the shadow of death, without any order,
and where the light is as darkness."'

11 Then answered Zophar the Naamathite, and said,
²'Should not the multitude of words be answered? And
should a man full of talk be justified? ³ Should thy lies make
men hold their peace? And when thou mockest, shall no man
make thee ashamed? ⁴For thou hast said, "My doctrine is
pure, and I am clean in thine eyes." ⁵But oh that God would
speak, and open his lips against thee; ⁶and that he would
shew thee the secrets of wisdom, that they are double to that
which is! Know therefore that God exacteth of thee less than
thine iniquity deserveth. ⁷Canst thou by searching find out
God? Canst thou find out the Almighty unto perfection? ⁸It
is as high as heaven; what canst thou do? Deeper than hell;
what canst thou know? ⁹The measure thereof is longer than
the earth, and broader than the sea. ¹⁰If he cut off, and shut
up, or gather together, then who can hinder him? ¹¹For he
knoweth vain men. He seeth wickedness also; will he not
then consider it? ¹²For vain man would be wise, though man
be born like a wild ass's colt. ¹³If thou prepare thine heart,
and stretch out thine hands toward him; ¹⁴if iniquity be in
thine hand, put it far away, and let not wickedness dwell in
thy tabernacles. ¹⁵For then shalt thou lift up thy face without
spot; yea, thou shalt be stedfast, and shalt not fear, ¹⁶because
thou shalt forget thy misery, and remember it as waters that
pass away. ¹⁷And thine age shall be clearer than the noonday; thou shalt shine forth, thou shalt be as the morning.

¹⁸And thou shalt be secure, because there is hope; yea, thou shalt dig about thee, and thou shalt take thy rest in safety. ¹⁹Also thou shalt lie down, and none shall make thee afraid; yea, many shall make suit unto thee. ²⁰But the eyes of the wicked shall fail, and they shall not escape, and their hope shall be as the giving up of the ghost.'

12 And Job answered and said,

²'No doubt but ye are the people,
   and wisdom shall die with you.
³But I have understanding as well as you;
   I am not inferior to you:
      yea, who knoweth not such things as these?
⁴I am as one mocked of his neighbour,
   I who calleth upon God, and he answereth him:
      the just upright man is laughed to scorn.
⁵He that is ready to slip with his feet
   is as a lamp despised in the thought of him
      that is at ease.
⁶The tabernacles of robbers prosper,
   and they that provoke God are secure;
      into whose hand God bringeth abundantly.
⁷But ask now the beasts, and they shall teach thee;
   and the fowls of the air, and they shall tell thee.
⁸Or speak to the earth, and it shall teach thee;
   and the fishes of the sea shall declare unto thee.
⁹Who knoweth not in all these that the hand of

the Lord hath wrought this?

¹⁰ In whose hand is the soul of every living thing,
and the breath of all mankind.

¹¹ Doth not the ear try words?
And the mouth taste his meat?

¹² With the ancient is wisdom;
and in length of days understanding.

¹³ With him is wisdom and strength,
he hath counsel and understanding.

¹⁴ Behold, he breaketh down,
and it cannot be built again;
he shutteth up a man,
and there can be no opening.

¹⁵ Behold, he withholdeth the waters, and they dry up;
also he sendeth them out,
and they overturn the earth.

¹⁶ With him is strength and wisdom;
the deceived and the deceiver are his.

¹⁷ He leadeth counsellors away spoiled,
and maketh the judges fools.

¹⁸ He looseth the bond of kings,
and girdeth their loins with a girdle.

¹⁹ He leadeth princes away spoiled,
and overthroweth the mighty.

²⁰ He removeth away the speech of the trusty,
and taketh away the understanding of the aged.

²¹ He poureth contempt upon princes,
and weakeneth the strength of the mighty.

²² He discovereth deep things out of darkness,
　　and bringeth out to light the shadow of death.
²³ He increaseth the nations, and destroyeth them;
　　he enlargeth the nations,
　　　　and straiteneth them again.
²⁴ He taketh away the heart of the chief of
　　the people of the earth,
　　　　and causeth them to wander
　　in a wilderness where there is no way.
²⁵ They grope in the dark without light, and
　　he maketh them to stagger like a drunken man.'

13 'Lo, mine eye hath seen all this,
　　mine ear hath heard and understood it.
² What ye know, the same do I know also:
　　I am not inferior unto you.
³ Surely I would speak to the Almighty,
　　and I desire to reason with God.
⁴ But ye are forgers of lies,
　　ye are all physicians of no value.
⁵ O that ye would altogether hold your peace!
　　And it should be your wisdom.
⁶ Hear now my reasoning,
　　and hearken to the pleadings of my lips.
⁷ Will ye speak wickedly for God?
　　And talk deceitfully for him?
⁸ Will ye accept his person? Will ye contend for God?
⁹ Is it good that he should search you out?

Or as one man mocketh another,
  do ye so mock him?
¹⁰ He will surely reprove you,
  if ye do secretly accept persons.
¹¹ Shall not his excellency make you afraid?
  And his dread fall upon you?
¹² Your remembrances are like unto ashes,
  your bodies to bodies of clay.
¹³ Hold your peace, let me alone, that I may speak,
  and let come on me what will.
¹⁴ Wherefore do I take my flesh in my teeth,
  and put my life in mine hand?
¹⁵ Though he slay me, yet will I trust in him;
  but I will maintain mine own ways before him.
¹⁶ He also shall be my salvation;
  for an hypocrite shall not come before him.
¹⁷ Hear diligently my speech,
  and my declaration with your ears.
¹⁸ Behold now I have ordered my cause;
  I know that I shall be justified.
¹⁹ Who is he that will plead with me?
  For now, if I hold my tongue,
    I shall give up the ghost.
²⁰ Only do not two things unto me;
  then will I not hide myself from thee.
²¹ Withdraw thine hand far from me;
  and let not thy dread make me afraid.
²² Then call thou, and I will answer;

or let me speak, and answer thou me.

²³ How many are mine iniquities and sins?
   Make me to know my transgression and my sin.
²⁴ Wherefore hidest thou thy face,
   and holdest me for thine enemy?
²⁵ Wilt thou break a leaf driven to and fro?
   And wilt thou pursue the dry stubble?
²⁶ For thou writest bitter things against me, and
   makest me to possess the iniquities of my youth.
²⁷ Thou puttest my feet also in the stocks,
   and lookest narrowly unto all my paths;
      thou settest a print upon the heels of my feet.
²⁸ And he, as a rotten thing, consumeth,
   as a garment that is moth eaten.'

14 'Man that is born of a woman is of few days,
   and full of trouble.
² He cometh forth like a flower, and is cut down;
   he fleeth also as a shadow, and continueth not.
³ And dost thou open thine eyes upon such an one,
   and bringest me into judgment with thee?
⁴ Who can bring a clean thing out of an unclean?
   Not one.
⁵ Seeing his days are determined,
   the number of his months are with thee,
      and thou hast appointed his bounds
   that he cannot pass,
⁶ turn from him, that he may rest,

till he shall accomplish, as an hireling, his day.
⁷ For there is hope of a tree, if it be cut down,
    that it will sprout again, and
        that the tender branch thereof will not cease.
⁸ Though the root thereof wax old in the earth,
    and the stock thereof die in the ground,
⁹ yet through the scent of water it will bud,
    and bring forth boughs like a plant.
¹⁰ But man dieth, and wasteth away;
    yea, man giveth up the ghost, and where is he?
¹¹ As the waters fail from the sea,
    and the flood decayeth and drieth up,
¹² so man lieth down, and riseth not;
    till the heavens be no more, they shall not awake,
        nor be raised out of their sleep.
¹³ O that thou wouldest hide me in the grave,
    that thou wouldest keep me secret,
        until thy wrath be past, that thou wouldest
    appoint me a set time, and remember me!
¹⁴ If a man die, shall he live again?
    all the days of my appointed time will I wait,
        till my change come.
¹⁵ Thou shalt call, and I will answer thee:
    thou wilt have a desire to the work of thine hands.
¹⁶ For now thou numberest my steps;
    dost thou not watch over my sin?
¹⁷ My transgression is sealed up in a bag,
    and thou sewest up mine iniquity.

¹⁸ And surely the mountain falling cometh to nought,
   and the rock is removed out of his place.
¹⁹ The waters wear the stones;
   thou washest away the things
      which grow out of the dust of the earth;
   and thou destroyest the hope of man.
²⁰ Thou prevailest for ever against him,
   and he passeth; thou changest his countenance,
      and sendest him away.
²¹ His sons come to honour, and he knoweth it not,
   and they are brought low,
      but he perceiveth it not of them.
²² But his flesh upon him shall have pain,
   and his soul within him shall mourn.'

15 Then answered Eliphaz the Temanite, and said, ² 'Should a wise man utter vain knowledge, and fill his belly with the east wind? ³ Should he reason with unprofitable talk? Or with speeches wherewith he can do no good? ⁴ Yea, thou castest off fear, and restrainest prayer before God. ⁵ For thy mouth uttereth thine iniquity, and thou choosest the tongue of the crafty. ⁶ Thine own mouth condemneth thee, and not I; yea, thine own lips testify against thee. ⁷ Art thou the first man that was born? Or wast thou made before the hills? ⁸ Hast thou heard the secret of God? And dost thou restrain wisdom to thyself? ⁹ What knowest thou, that we know not? What understandest thou, which is not in us? ¹⁰ With us are both the grayheaded and very aged men, much elder than thy father. ¹¹ Are

the consolations of God small with thee? Is there any secret thing with thee? ¹²Why doth thine heart carry thee away? And what do thy eyes wink at, ¹³ that thou turnest thy spirit against God, and lettest such words go out of thy mouth? ¹⁴What is man, that he should be clean? And he which is born of a woman, that he should be righteous? ¹⁵Behold, he putteth no trust in his saints; yea, the heavens are not clean in his sight. ¹⁶How much more abominable and filthy is man, which drinketh iniquity like water? ¹⁷I will shew thee, hear me; and that which I have seen I will declare; ¹⁸which wise men have told from their fathers, and have not hid it: ¹⁹ unto whom alone the earth was given, and no stranger passed among them. ²⁰The wicked man travaileth with pain all his days, and the number of years is hidden to the oppressor. ²¹A dreadful sound is in his ears; in prosperity the destroyer shall come upon him. ²²He believeth not that he shall return out of darkness, and he is waited for of the sword. ²³ He wandereth abroad for bread, saying, "Where is it?" He knoweth that the day of darkness is ready at his hand. ²⁴Trouble and anguish shall make him afraid; they shall prevail against him, as a king ready to the battle. ²⁵For he stretcheth out his hand against God, and strengtheneth himself against the Almighty. ²⁶He runneth upon him, even on his neck, upon the thick bosses of his bucklers; ²⁷ because he covereth his face with his fatness, and maketh collops of fat on his flanks. ²⁸And he dwelleth in desolate cities, and in houses which no man inhabiteth, which are ready to become heaps. ²⁹He shall not be rich, neither shall his substance continue, neither shall he prolong the perfection thereof upon the earth. ³⁰ He shall not depart out of darkness; the flame shall dry up his branches, and by the breath of his mouth shall he go away. ³¹ Let not him that is deceived trust in vanity; for vanity shall be his recompence. ³² It shall be accomplished before his time, and his branch shall not be green. ³³ He shall shake off his unripe grape as the vine, and shall cast off his flower as the olive. ³⁴ For the congregation of hypocrites shall be desolate, and fire shall consume the tabernacles of bribery. ³⁵ They conceive mischief, and bring forth vanity, and their belly prepareth deceit.'

16 Then Job answered and said,

² 'I have heard many such things:
   miserable comforters are ye all.
³ Shall vain words have an end?
   Or what emboldeneth thee that thou answerest?
⁴ I also could speak as ye do;
   if your soul were in my soul's stead,
      I could heap up words against you,
   and shake mine head at you.
⁵ But I would strengthen you with my mouth, and
   the moving of my lips should asswage your grief.
⁶ Though I speak, my grief is not asswaged;
   and though I forbear, what am I eased?
⁷ But now he hath made me weary;
   thou hast made desolate all my company.
⁸ And thou hast filled me with wrinkles,

which is a witness against me; and my leanness
    rising up in me beareth witness to my face.
⁹ He teareth me in his wrath, who hateth me;
    he gnasheth upon me with his teeth;
        mine enemy sharpeneth his eyes upon me.
¹⁰ They have gaped upon me with their mouth;
    they have smitten me upon
        the cheek reproachfully; they have gathered
    themselves together against me.
¹¹ God hath delivered me to the ungodly,
    and turned me over into the hands of the wicked.
¹² I was at ease, but he hath broken me asunder;
    he hath also taken me by my neck, and shaken
        me to pieces, and set me up for his mark.
¹³ His archers compass me round about,
    he cleaveth my reins asunder, and doth not spare;
        he poureth out my gall upon the ground.
¹⁴ He breaketh me with breach upon breach,
    he runneth upon me like a giant.
¹⁵ I have sewed sackcloth upon my skin,
    and defiled my horn in the dust.
¹⁶ My face is foul with weeping,
    and on my eyelids is the shadow of death;
¹⁷ not for any injustice in mine hands,
    also my prayer is pure.
¹⁸ O earth, cover not thou my blood,
    and let my cry have no place.
¹⁹ Also now, behold, my witness is in heaven,

and my record is on high.
²⁰ My friends scorn me;
    but mine eye poureth out tears unto God.
²¹ O that one might plead for a man with God,
    as a man pleadeth for his neighbour!
²² When a few years are come,
    then I shall go the way whence I shall not return.'

17 'My breath is corrupt, my days are extinct,
    the graves are ready for me.
² Are there not mockers with me? And doth not
    mine eye continue in their provocation?
³ Lay down now, put me in a surety with thee;
    who is he that will strike hands with me?
⁴ For thou hast hid their heart from understanding;
    therefore shalt thou not exalt them.
⁵ He that speaketh flattery to his friends,
    even the eyes of his children shall fail.
⁶ He hath made me also a byword of the people;
    and aforetime I was as a tabret.
⁷ Mine eye also is dim by reason of sorrow,
    and all my members are as a shadow.
⁸ Upright men shall be astonied at this,
    and the innocent shall stir up himself
        against the hypocrite.
⁹ The righteous also shall hold on his way,
    and he that hath clean hands
        shall be stronger and stronger.

¹⁰ But as for you all, do ye return, and come now;
   for I cannot find one wise man among you.
¹¹ My days are past, my purposes are broken off,
   even the thoughts of my heart.
¹² They change the night into day;
   the light is short because of darkness.
¹³ If I wait, the grave is mine house;
   I have made my bed in the darkness.
¹⁴ I have said to corruption, "Thou art my father;"
   to the worm, "Thou art my mother, and my sister."
¹⁵ And where is now my hope?
   As for my hope, who shall see it?
¹⁶ They shall go down to the bars of the pit,
   when our rest together is in the dust.'

18 Then answered Bildad the Shuhite, and said, ² 'How long will it be ere ye make an end of words? Mark, and afterwards we will speak. ³ Wherefore are we counted as beasts, and reputed vile in your sight? ⁴ He teareth himself in his anger; shall the earth be forsaken for thee? And shall the rock be removed out of his place? ⁵ Yea, the light of the wicked shall be put out, and the spark of his fire shall not shine. ⁶ The light shall be dark in his tabernacle, and his candle shall be put out with him. ⁷ The steps of his strength shall be straitened, and his own counsel shall cast him down. ⁸ For he is cast into a net by his own feet, and he walketh upon a snare. ⁹ The gin shall take him by the heel, and the robber shall prevail against him. ¹⁰ The snare is laid for him in the ground,

and a trap for him in the way. ¹¹ Terrors shall make him afraid on every side, and shall drive him to his feet. ¹² His strength shall be hungerbitten, and destruction shall be ready at his side. ¹³ It shall devour the strength of his skin; even the first-born of death shall devour his strength. ¹⁴ His confidence shall be rooted out of his tabernacle, and it shall bring him to the king of terrors. ¹⁵ It shall dwell in his tabernacle, because it is none of his; brimstone shall be scattered upon his habitation. ¹⁶ His roots shall be dried up beneath, and above shall his branch be cut off. ¹⁷ His remembrance shall perish from the earth, and he shall have no name in the street. ¹⁸ He shall be driven from light into darkness, and chased out of the world. ¹⁹ He shall neither have son nor nephew among his people, nor any remaining in his dwellings. ²⁰ They that come after him shall be astonied at his day, as they that went before were affrighted. ²¹ Surely such are the dwellings of the wicked, and this is the place of him that knoweth not God.'

19

Then Job answered and said,

² 'How long will ye vex my soul,
and break me in pieces with words?
³ These ten times have ye reproached me;
ye are not ashamed that ye make
yourselves strange to me.
⁴ And be it indeed that I have erred,
mine error remaineth with myself.
⁵ If indeed ye will magnify yourselves against me,

and plead against me my reproach,

⁶ know now that God hath overthrown me,

and hath compassed me with his net.

⁷ Behold, I cry out of wrong, but I am not heard;

I cry aloud, but there is no judgment.

⁸ He hath fenced up my way that I cannot pass,

and he hath set darkness in my paths.

⁹ He hath stripped me of my glory,

and taken the crown from my head.

¹⁰ He hath destroyed me on every side,

and I am gone;

and mine hope hath he removed like a tree.

¹¹ He hath also kindled his wrath against me, and

he counteth me unto him as one of his enemies.

¹² His troops come together,

and raise up their way against me,

and encamp round about my tabernacle.

¹³ He hath put my brethren far from me, and

mine acquaintance are verily estranged from me.

¹⁴ My kinsfolk have failed,

and my familiar friends have forgotten me.

¹⁵ They that dwell in mine house,

and my maids, count me for a stranger:

I am an alien in their sight.

¹⁶ I called my servant, and he gave me no answer;

I intreated him with my mouth.

¹⁷ My breath is strange to my wife, though I intreated

for the children's sake of mine own body.

¹⁸ Yea, young children despised me;

   I arose, and they spake against me.
¹⁹ All my inward friends abhorred me:

   and they whom I loved are turned against me.
²⁰ My bone cleaveth to my skin and to my flesh,

   and I am escaped with the skin of my teeth.
²¹ Have pity upon me, have pity upon me,

   O ye my friends;

      for the hand of God hath touched me.
²² Why do ye persecute me as God,

   and are not satisfied with my flesh?
²³ 'Oh that my words were now written!

   Oh that they were printed in a book!
²⁴ That they were graven with an iron pen

   and lead in the rock for ever!
²⁵ For I know that my redeemer liveth, and that

   he shall stand at the latter day upon the earth;
²⁶ and though after my skin worms destroy this body,

   yet in my flesh shall I see God,
²⁷ whom I shall see for myself,

   and mine eyes shall behold, and not another,

      though my reins be consumed within me.
²⁸ But ye should say, "Why persecute we him,

   seeing the root of the matter is found in me?"
²⁹ Be ye afraid of the sword;

   for wrath bringeth the punishments of the sword,

      that ye may know there is a judgment.'

20 Then answered Zophar the Naamathite, and said, ² "Therefore do my thoughts cause me to answer, and for this I make haste. ³ I have heard the check of my reproach, and the spirit of my understanding causeth me to answer. ⁴ Knowest thou not this of old, since man was placed upon earth, ⁵ that the triumphing of the wicked is short, and the joy of the hypocrite but for a moment? ⁶ Though his excellency mount up to the heavens, and his head reach unto the clouds, ⁷ yet he shall perish for ever like his own dung; they which have seen him shall say, "Where is he?" ⁸ He shall fly away as a dream, and shall not be found; yea, he shall be chased away as a vision of the night. ⁹ The eye also which saw him shall see him no more; neither shall his place any more behold him. ¹⁰ His children shall seek to please the poor, and his hands shall restore their goods. ¹¹ His bones are full of the sin of his youth, which shall lie down with him in the dust. ¹² Though wickedness be sweet in his mouth, though he hide it under his tongue; ¹³ though he spare it, and forsake it not, but keep it still within his mouth; ¹⁴ yet his meat in his bowels is turned; it is the gall of asps within him. ¹⁵ He hath swallowed down riches, and he shall vomit them up again: God shall cast them out of his belly. ¹⁶ He shall suck the poison of asps: the viper's tongue shall slay him. ¹⁷ He shall not see the rivers, the floods, the brooks of honey and butter. ¹⁸ That which he laboured for shall he restore, and shall not swallow it down; according to his substance shall the restitution be, and he shall not rejoice therein. ¹⁹ Because he hath oppressed and hath forsaken the poor, because he hath violently taken away an house

which he builded not, ²⁰ surely he shall not feel quietness in his belly; he shall not save of that which he desired. ²¹ There shall none of his meat be left; therefore shall no man look for his goods. ²² In the fulness of his sufficiency he shall be in straits; every hand of the wicked shall come upon him. ²³ When he is about to fill his belly, God shall cast the fury of his wrath upon him, and shall rain it upon him while he is eating. ²⁴ He shall flee from the iron weapon, and the bow of steel shall strike him through. ²⁵ It is drawn, and cometh out of the body; yea, the glittering sword cometh out of his gall: terrors are upon him. ²⁶ All darkness shall be hid in his secret places; a fire not blown shall consume him; it shall go ill with him that is left in his tabernacle. ²⁷ The heaven shall reveal his iniquity; and the earth shall rise up against him. ²⁸ The increase of his house shall depart, and his goods shall flow away in the day of his wrath. ²⁹ This is the portion of a wicked man from God, and the heritage appointed unto him by God.'

21

But Job answered and said,

² 'Hear diligently my speech,
    and let this be your consolations.
³ Suffer me that I may speak;
    and after that I have spoken, mock on.
⁴ As for me, is my complaint to man?
    And if it were so,
        why should not my spirit be troubled?
⁵ Mark me, and be astonished,

and lay your hand upon your mouth.
⁶ Even when I remember I am afraid,
and trembling taketh hold on my flesh.
⁷ Wherefore do the wicked live, become old,
yea, are mighty in power?
⁸ Their seed is established in their sight with them,
and their offspring before their eyes.
⁹ Their houses are safe from fear;
neither is the rod of God upon them.
¹⁰ Their bull gendereth, and faileth not;
their cow calveth, and casteth not her calf.
¹¹ They send forth their little ones like a flock,
and their children dance.
¹² They take the timbrel and harp,
and rejoice at the sound of the organ.
¹³ They spend their days in wealth,
and in a moment go down to the grave.
¹⁴ Therefore they say unto God,
"Depart from us; for we desire not
the knowledge of thy ways.
¹⁵ What is the Almighty, that we should serve him?
And what profit should we have,
if we pray unto him?"
¹⁶ Lo, their good is not in their hand:
the counsel of the wicked is far from me.
¹⁷ How oft is the candle of the wicked put out!
And how oft cometh their destruction upon them!
God distributeth sorrows in his anger.

¹⁸ They are as stubble before the wind,
    and as chaff that the storm carrieth away.
¹⁹ God layeth up his iniquity for his children;
    he rewardeth him, and he shall know it.
²⁰ His eyes shall see his destruction,
    and he shall drink of the wrath of the Almighty.
²¹ For what pleasure hath he in his house after him,
    when the number of his months
        is cut off in the midst?
²² Shall any teach God knowledge,
    seeing he judgeth those that are high?
²³ One dieth in his full strength,
    being wholly at ease and quiet.
²⁴ His breasts are full of milk,
    and his bones are moistened with marrow.
²⁵ And another dieth in the bitterness of his soul,
    and never eateth with pleasure.
²⁶ They shall lie down alike in the dust,
    and the worms shall cover them.
²⁷ Behold, I know your thoughts,
    and the devices which ye wrongfully
        imagine against me.
²⁸ For ye say, "Where is the house of the prince?
    And where are the dwelling places of the wicked?"
²⁹ Have ye not asked them that go by the way?
    And do ye not know their tokens,
³⁰ that the wicked is reserved to the day of destruction?
    They shall be brought forth to the day of wrath.

³¹ Who shall declare his way to his face?
    And who shall repay him what he hath done?
³² Yet shall he be brought to the grave,
    and shall remain in the tomb.
³³ The clods of the valley shall be sweet unto him,
    and every man shall draw after him,
        as there are innumerable before him.
³⁴ How then comfort ye me in vain,
    seeing in your answers
        there remaineth falsehood?'

22 Then Eliphaz the Temanite answered and said, ² 'Can a man be profitable unto God, as he that is wise may be profitable unto himself? ³ Is it any pleasure to the Almighty, that thou art righteous? Or is it gain to him, that thou makest thy ways perfect? ⁴ Will he reprove thee for fear of thee? Will he enter with thee into judgment? ⁵ Is not thy wickedness great? And thine iniquities infinite? ⁶ For thou hast taken a pledge from thy brother for nought, and stripped the naked of their clothing. ⁷ Thou hast not given water to the weary to drink, and thou hast withholden bread from the hungry. ⁸ But as for the mighty man, he had the earth; and the honourable man dwelt in it. ⁹ Thou hast sent widows away empty, and the arms of the fatherless have been broken. ¹⁰ Therefore snares are round about thee, and sudden fear troubleth thee, ¹¹ Or darkness, that thou canst not see; and abundance of waters cover thee. ¹² Is not God in the height of heaven? And behold the height of the stars, how high they are! ¹³ And thou

sayest, "How doth God know? Can he judge through the dark cloud?" ¹⁴ Thick clouds are a covering to him, that he seeth not; and he walketh in the circuit of heaven. ¹⁵ Hast thou marked the old way which wicked men have trodden? ¹⁶ Which were cut down out of time, whose foundation was overflown with a flood; ¹⁷ which said unto God, "Depart from us" and "What can the Almighty do for them?" ¹⁸ Yet he filled their houses with good things; but the counsel of the wicked is far from me. ¹⁹ The righteous see it, and are glad; and the innocent laugh them to scorn. ²⁰ Whereas our substance is not cut down, but the remnant of them the fire consumeth. ²¹ Acquaint now thyself with him, and be at peace; thereby good shall come unto thee. ²² Receive, I pray thee, the law from his mouth, and lay up his words in thine heart. ²³ If thou return to the Almighty, thou shalt be built up; thou shalt put away iniquity far from thy tabernacles. ²⁴ Then shalt thou lay up gold as dust, and the gold of Ophir as the stones of the brooks. ²⁵ Yea, the Almighty shall be thy defence, and thou shalt have plenty of silver. ²⁶ For then shalt thou have thy delight in the Almighty, and shalt lift up thy face unto God. ²⁷ Thou shalt make thy prayer unto him, and he shall hear thee, and thou shalt pay thy vows. ²⁸ Thou shalt also decree a thing, and it shall be established unto thee; and the light shall shine upon thy ways. ²⁹ When men are cast down, then thou shalt say, "There is lifting up"; and he shall save the humble person. ³⁰ He shall deliver the island of the innocent; and it is delivered by the pureness of thine hands.'

23

Then Job answered and said,

² 'Even to day is my complaint bitter;
  my stroke is heavier than my groaning.
³ Oh that I knew where I might find him!
  That I might come even to his seat!
⁴ I would order my cause before him,
  and fill my mouth with arguments.
⁵ I would know the words which he would answer me,
  and understand what he would say unto me.
⁶ Will he plead against me with his great power?
  No, but he would put strength in me.
⁷ There the righteous might dispute with him;
  so should I be delivered for ever from my judge.
⁸ Behold, I go forward, but he is not there;
  and backward, but I cannot perceive him;
⁹ on the left hand, where he doth work,
  but I cannot behold him;
    he hideth himself on the right hand,
  that I cannot see him.
¹⁰ But he knoweth the way that I take;
  when he hath tried me, I shall come forth as gold.
¹¹ My foot hath held his steps;
  his way have I kept, and not declined.
¹² Neither have I gone back from
  the commandment of his lips;
    I have esteemed the words of his mouth
  more than my necessary food.

¹³ But he is in one mind, and who can turn him?
   And what his soul desireth, even that he doeth.
¹⁴ For he performeth the thing that is appointed for me;
   and many such things are with him.
¹⁵ Therefore am I troubled at his presence;
   when I consider, I am afraid of him.
¹⁶ For God maketh my heart soft,
   and the Almighty troubleth me,
¹⁷ Because I was not cut off before the darkness,
   neither hath he covered the darkness from my face.'

24 'Why, seeing times are not hidden from the Almighty,
   do they that know him not see his days?
² Some remove the landmarks;
   they violently take away flocks, and feed thereof.
³ They drive away the ass of the fatherless,
   they take the widow's ox for a pledge.
⁴ They turn the needy out of the way;
   the poor of the earth hide themselves together.
⁵ Behold, as wild asses in the desert,
   go they forth to their work,
      rising betimes for a prey;
   the wilderness yieldeth food for them
      and for their children.
⁶ They reap every one his corn in the field;
   and they gather the vintage of the wicked.
⁷ They cause the naked to lodge without clothing,
   that they have no covering in the cold.

⁸ They are wet with the showers of the mountains,
  and embrace the rock for want of a shelter.
⁹ They pluck the fatherless from the breast,
  and take a pledge of the poor.
¹⁰ They cause him to go naked without clothing,
  and they take away the sheaf from the hungry;
¹¹ which make oil within their walls,
  and tread their winepresses, and suffer thirst.
¹² Men groan from out of the city,
  and the soul of the wounded crieth out;
    yet God layeth not folly to them.
¹³ They are of those that rebel against the light;
  they know not the ways thereof,
    nor abide in the paths thereof.
¹⁴ The murderer rising with the light killeth the poor
  and needy, and in the night is as a thief.
¹⁵ The eye also of the adulterer waiteth for
  the twilight, saying, "No eye shall see me;"
    and disguiseth his face.
¹⁶ In the dark they dig through houses,
  which they had marked for themselves
    in the daytime;
  they know not the light.
¹⁷ For the morning is to them
  even as the shadow of death;
    if one know them,
  they are in the terrors of the shadow of death.
¹⁸ He is swift as the waters;

their portion is cursed in the earth;
>> he beholdeth not the way of the vineyards.
¹⁹ Drought and heat consume the snow waters;
>> so doth the grave those which have sinned.
²⁰ The womb shall forget him;
>> the worm shall feed sweetly on him;
>> he shall be no more remembered;
>> and wickedness shall be broken as a tree.
²¹ He evil entreateth the barren that beareth not;
>> and doeth not good to the widow.
²² He draweth also the mighty with his power;
>> he riseth up, and no man is sure of life.
²³ Though it be given him to be in safety,
>> whereon he resteth;
>> yet his eyes are upon their ways.
²⁴ They are exalted for a little while,
>> but are gone and brought low;
>> they are taken out of the way as all other,
>> and cut off as the tops of the ears of corn.
²⁵ And if it be not so now, who will make me a liar,
>> and make my speech nothing worth?'

25 Then answered Bildad the Shuhite, and said, ² 'Dominion and fear are with him, he maketh peace in his high places. ³ Is there any number of his armies? And upon whom doth not his light arise? ⁴ How then can man be justified with God? Or how can he be clean that is born of a woman? ⁵ Behold even to the moon, and it shineth not; yea, the stars are not pure in his sight. ⁶How much less man, that is a worm? And the son of man, which is a worm?'

26 But Job answered and said,

²'How hast thou helped him that is without power?
  How savest thou the arm that hath no strength?
³How hast thou counselled him that hath no wisdom?
    And how hast thou plentifully declared
    the thing as it is?
⁴To whom hast thou uttered words?
  And whose spirit came from thee?
⁵Dead things are formed from under the waters,
  and the inhabitants thereof.
⁶Hell is naked before him,
  and destruction hath no covering.
⁷He stretcheth out the north over the empty place,
  and hangeth the earth upon nothing.
⁸He bindeth up the waters in his thick clouds;
  and the cloud is not rent under them.
⁹He holdeth back the face of his throne,
  and spreadeth his cloud upon it.
¹⁰He hath compassed the waters with bounds,
  until the day and night come to an end.
¹¹The pillars of heaven tremble
  and are astonished at his reproof.
¹²He divideth the sea with his power, and by his
  understanding he smiteth through the proud.

¹³ By his spirit he hath garnished the heavens;
   his hand hath formed the crooked serpent.
¹⁴ Lo, these are parts of his ways;
   but how little a portion is heard of him?
      But the thunder of his power
   who can understand?'

27 Moreover Job continued his parable, and said,

² 'As God liveth, who hath taken away my judgment,
   and the Almighty, who hath vexed my soul,
³ all the while my breath is in me,
   and the spirit of God is in my nostrils,
⁴ my lips shall not speak wickedness,
   nor my tongue utter deceit.
⁵ God forbid that I should justify you;
   till I die I will not remove mine integrity from me.
⁶ My righteousness I hold fast, and will not let it go;
   my heart shall not reproach me so long as I live.
⁷ Let mine enemy be as the wicked, and
   he that riseth up against me as the unrighteous.
⁸ For what is the hope of the hypocrite,
   though he hath gained,
      when God taketh away his soul?
⁹ Will God hear his cry when trouble
   cometh upon him?
¹⁰ Will he delight himself in the Almighty?
   Will he always call upon God?

¹¹ I will teach you by the hand of God;
    that which is with the Almighty will I not conceal.
¹² Behold, all ye yourselves have seen it;
    why then are ye thus altogether vain?
¹³ This is the portion of a wicked man with God,
    and the heritage of oppressors,
       which they shall receive of the Almighty.
¹⁴ If his children be multiplied, it is for the sword;
    and his offspring shall not be satisfied with bread.
¹⁵ Those that remain of him shall be buried in death;
    and his widows shall not weep.
¹⁶ Though he heap up silver as the dust,
    and prepare raiment as the clay,
¹⁷ he may prepare it, but the just shall put it on,
    and the innocent shall divide the silver.
¹⁸ He buildeth his house as a moth,
    and as a booth that the keeper maketh.
¹⁹ The rich man shall lie down,
    but he shall not be gathered;
       he openeth his eyes, and he is not.
²⁰ Terrors take hold on him as waters,
    a tempest stealeth him away in the night.
²¹ The east wind carrieth him away, and he departeth;
    and as a storm hurleth him out of his place.
²² For God shall cast upon him, and not spare;
    he would fain flee out of his hand.
²³ Men shall clap their hands at him,
    and shall hiss him out of his place.'

28

'Surely there is a vein for the silver,
and a place for gold where they fine it.
² Iron is taken out of the earth,
and brass is molten out of the stone.
³ He setteth an end to darkness,
and searcheth out all perfection;
the stones of darkness, and the shadow of death.
⁴ The flood breaketh out from the inhabitant,
even the waters forgotten of the foot;
they are dried up,
they are gone away from men.
⁵ As for the earth, out of it cometh bread;
and under it is turned up as it were fire.
⁶ The stones of it are the place of sapphires;
and it hath dust of gold.
⁷ There is a path which no fowl knoweth,
and which the vulture's eye hath not seen;
⁸ the lion's whelps have not trodden it,
nor the fierce lion passed by it.
⁹ He putteth forth his hand upon the rock;
he overturneth the mountains by the roots.
¹⁰ He cutteth out rivers among the rocks;
and his eye seeth every precious thing.
¹¹ He bindeth the floods from overflowing;
and the thing that is hid bringeth he forth to light.
¹² But where shall wisdom be found?
And where is the place of understanding?
¹³ Man knoweth not the price thereof;

neither is it found in the land of the living.

¹⁴ The depth saith, "It is not in me;"
and the sea saith, "It is not with me."
¹⁵ It cannot be gotten for gold, neither shall silver
be weighed for the price thereof.
¹⁶ It cannot be valued with the gold of Ophir,
with the precious onyx, or the sapphire.
¹⁷ The gold and the crystal cannot equal it;
and the exchange of it
shall not be for jewels of fine gold.
¹⁸ No mention shall be made of coral, or of pearls,
for the price of wisdom is above rubies.
¹⁹ The topaz of Ethiopia shall not equal it,
neither shall it be valued with pure gold.
²⁰ Whence then cometh wisdom?
And where is the place of understanding,
²¹ seeing it is hid from the eyes of all living,
and kept close from the fowls of the air?
²² Destruction and death say,
"We have heard the fame thereof with our ears."
²³ God understandeth the way thereof,
and he knoweth the place thereof.
²⁴ For he looketh to the ends of the earth,
and seeth under the whole heaven,
²⁵ to make the weight for the winds;
and he weigheth the waters by measure.
²⁶ When he made a decree for the rain,
and a way for the lightning of the thunder,

²⁷ then did he see it, and declare it;
    he prepared it, yea, and searched it out.
²⁸ And unto man he said,
    "Behold, the fear of the Lord, that is wisdom;
        and to depart from evil is understanding."'

29

Moreover Job continued his parable, and said,

² 'Oh that I were as in months past,
    as in the days when God preserved me;
³ when his candle shined upon my head,
    and when by his light I walked through darkness,
⁴ as I was in the days of my youth,
    when the secret of God was upon my tabernacle;
⁵ when the Almighty was yet with me,
    when my children were about me;
⁶ when I washed my steps with butter,
    and the rock poured me out rivers of oil;
⁷ when I went out to the gate through the city,
    when I prepared my seat in the street,
⁸ the young men saw me, and hid themselves;
    and the aged arose, and stood up.
⁹ The princes refrained talking,
    and laid their hand on their mouth.
¹⁰ The nobles held their peace, and their tongue
    cleaved to the roof of their mouth.
¹¹ When the ear heard me, then it blessed me;
    and when the eye saw me, it gave witness to me;

¹² because I delivered the poor that cried, and
    the fatherless, and him that had none to help him.
¹³ The blessing of him that was ready to perish
    came upon me;
        and I caused the widow's heart to sing for joy.
¹⁴ I put on righteousness, and it clothed me;
    my judgment was as a robe and a diadem.
¹⁵ I was eyes to the blind, and feet was I to the lame.
¹⁶ I was a father to the poor;
    and the cause which I knew not I searched out.
¹⁷ And I brake the jaws of the wicked,
    and plucked the spoil out of his teeth.
¹⁸ Then I said, "I shall die in my nest,
    and I shall multiply my days as the sand."
¹⁹ My root was spread out by the waters,
    and the dew lay all night upon my branch.
²⁰ My glory was fresh in me,
    and my bow was renewed in my hand.
²¹ Unto me men gave ear, and waited,
    and kept silence at my counsel.
²² After my words they spake not again;
    and my speech dropped upon them.
²³ And they waited for me as for the rain;
    and they opened their mouth wide
        as for the latter rain.
²⁴ If I laughed on them, they believed it not;
    and the light of my countenance
        they cast not down.

²⁵ I chose out their way, and sat chief,
and dwelt as a king in the army,
as one that comforteth the mourners.'

30

'But now they that are younger than I
have me in derision,
whose fathers I would have disdained
to have set with the dogs of my flock.
² Yea, whereto might the strength of their hands
profit me, in whom old age was perished?
³ For want and famine they were solitary;
fleeing into the wilderness in former time
desolate and waste;
⁴ who cut up mallows by the bushes,
and juniper roots for their meat.
⁵ They were driven forth from among men
(they cried after them as after a thief)
⁶ to dwell in the clifts of the valleys,
in caves of the earth, and in the rocks.
⁷ Among the bushes they brayed;
under the nettles they were gathered together.
⁸ They were children of fools,
yea, children of base men;
they were viler than the earth.
⁹ And now am I their song, yea, I am their byword.
¹⁰ They abhor me, they flee far from me,
and spare not to spit in my face.
¹¹ Because he hath loosed my cord, and afflicted me,

they have also let loose the bridle before me.
¹²Upon my right hand rise the youth;
    they push away my feet,
        and they raise up against me
    the ways of their destruction.
¹³They mar my path, they set forward my calamity,
    they have no helper.
¹⁴They came upon me as a wide breaking in of waters;
    in the desolation they rolled themselves upon me.
¹⁵Terrors are turned upon me;
    they pursue my soul as the wind;
        and my welfare passeth away as a cloud.
¹⁶And now my soul is poured out upon me;
    the days of affliction have taken hold upon me.
¹⁷My bones are pierced in me in the night season;
    and my sinews take no rest.
¹⁸By the great force of my disease
    is my garment changed;
        it bindeth me about as the collar of my coat.
¹⁹He hath cast me into the mire,
    and I am become like dust and ashes.
²⁰I cry unto thee, and thou dost not hear me:
    I stand up, and thou regardest me not.
²¹Thou art become cruel to me;
    with thy strong hand
        thou opposest thyself against me.
²²Thou liftest me up to the wind;
    thou causest me to ride upon it,

and dissolvest my substance.
²³ For I know that thou wilt bring me to death,
    and to the house appointed for all living.
²⁴ Howbeit he will not stretch out
    his hand to the grave,
        though they cry in his destruction.
²⁵ Did not I weep for him that was in trouble?
    Was not my soul grieved for the poor?
²⁶ When I looked for good, then evil came unto me;
    and when I waited for light, there came darkness.
²⁷ My bowels boiled, and rested not;
    the days of affliction prevented me.
²⁸ I went mourning without the sun;
    I stood up, and I cried in the congregation.
²⁹ I am a brother to dragons,
    and a companion to owls.
³⁰ My skin is black upon me,
    and my bones are burned with heat.
³¹ My harp also is turned to mourning,
    and my organ into the voice of them that weep.'

31 'I made a covenant with mine eyes;
    why then should I think upon a maid?
² For what portion of God is there from above?
    And what inheritance
        of the Almighty from on high?
³ Is not destruction to the wicked?
    And a strange punishment

to the workers of iniquity?
⁴ Doth not he see my ways, and count all my steps?
⁵ If I have walked with vanity,
or if my foot hath hasted to deceit,
⁶ let me be weighed in an even balance,
that God may know mine integrity.
⁷ If my step hath turned out of the way,
and mine heart walked after mine eyes,
and if any blot hath cleaved to mine hands,
⁸ then let me sow, and let another eat;
yea, let my offspring be rooted out.
⁹ If mine heart have been deceived by a woman,
or if I have laid wait at my neighbour's door,
¹⁰ then let my wife grind unto another,
and let others bow down upon her.
¹¹ For this is an heinous crime;
yea, it is an iniquity to be punished by the judges.
¹² For it is a fire that consumeth to destruction,
and would root out all mine increase.
¹³ If I did despise the cause of my manservant
or of my maidservant,
when they contended with me,
¹⁴ what then shall I do when God riseth up?
And when he visiteth, what shall I answer him?
¹⁵ Did not he that made me in the womb make him?
And did not one fashion us in the womb?
¹⁶ If I have withheld the poor from their desire,
or have caused the eyes of the widow to fail;

¹⁷or have eaten my morsel myself alone,
  and the fatherless hath not eaten thereof
¹⁸(for from my youth he was brought up with me,
    as with a father,
      and I have guided her
      from my mother's womb);
¹⁹if I have seen any perish for want of clothing,
    or any poor without covering;
²⁰if his loins have not blessed me,
    and if he were not warmed
      with the fleece of my sheep;
²¹if I have lifted up my hand against the fatherless,
    when I saw my help in the gate:
²²then let mine arm fall from my shoulder blade,
    and mine arm be broken from the bone.
²³For destruction from God was a terror to me,
    and by reason of his highness I could not endure.
²⁴If I have made gold my hope,
    or have said to the fine gold,
      "Thou art my confidence;"
²⁵if I rejoiced because my wealth was great,
    and because mine hand had gotten much;
²⁶if I beheld the sun when it shined,
    or the moon walking in brightness;
²⁷and my heart hath been secretly enticed,
    or my mouth hath kissed my hand:
²⁸this also were an iniquity
    to be punished by the judge;

for I should have denied the God that is above.

²⁹ If I rejoiced at the destruction of him that hated me,
    or lifted up myself when evil found him,

³⁰ neither have I suffered my mouth to sin
    by wishing a curse to his soul.

³¹ If the men of my tabernacle said not,
    "Oh that we had of his flesh!"
        we cannot be satisfied.

³² The stranger did not lodge in the street;
    but I opened my doors to the traveller.

³³ If I covered my transgressions as Adam,
    by hiding mine iniquity in my bosom,

³⁴ did I fear a great multitude,
    or did the contempt of families terrify me,
        that I kept silence,
    and went not out of the door?

³⁵ Oh that one would hear me!
    Behold, my desire is that the Almighty
        would answer me,
    and that mine adversary had written a book.

³⁶ Surely I would take it upon my shoulder,
    and bind it as a crown to me.

³⁷ I would declare unto him the number of my steps;
    as a prince would I go near unto him.

³⁸ If my land cry against me,
    or that the furrows likewise thereof complain;

³⁹ if I have eaten the fruits thereof without money,
    or have caused the owners thereof to lose their life,

⁴⁰ let thistles grow instead of wheat,
    and cockle instead of barley.'

The words of Job are ended.

32 So these three men ceased to answer Job, because he was righteous in his own eyes. ²Then was kindled the wrath of Elihu the son of Barachel the Buzite, of the kindred of Ram; against Job was his wrath kindled, because he justified himself rather than God. ³Also against his three friends was his wrath kindled, because they had found no answer, and yet had condemned Job. ⁴Now Elihu had waited till Job had spoken, because they were elder than he. ⁵When Elihu saw that there was no answer in the mouth of these three men, then his wrath was kindled. ⁶And Elihu the son of Barachel the Buzite answered and said,

'I am young, and ye are very old; wherefore I was afraid, and durst not shew you mine opinion. ⁷I said, "Days should speak, and multitude of years should teach wisdom." ⁸But there is a spirit in man; and the inspiration of the Almighty giveth them understanding. ⁹Great men are not always wise; neither do the aged understand judgment. ¹⁰Therefore I said, "Hearken to me; I also will shew mine opinion."

¹¹'Behold, I waited for your words; I gave ear to your reasons, whilst ye searched out what to say. ¹²Yea, I attended unto you, and, behold, there was none of you that convinced Job, or that answered his words: ¹³lest ye should say, "We have found out wisdom: God thrusteth him down, not man."

¹⁴ Now he hath not directed his words against me; neither will I answer him with your speeches.

¹⁵ 'They were amazed, they answered no more; they left off speaking. ¹⁶ When I had waited (for they spake not, but stood still, and answered no more), ¹⁷ I said, "I will answer also my part, I also will shew mine opinion." ¹⁸ For I am full of matter; the spirit within me constraineth me. ¹⁹ Behold, my belly is as wine which hath no vent; it is ready to burst like new bottles. ²⁰ I will speak, that I may be refreshed; I will open my lips and answer. ²¹ Let me not, I pray you, accept any man's person, neither let me give flattering titles unto man. ²² For I know not to give flattering titles; in so doing my maker would soon take me away.

33

'Wherefore, Job, I pray thee, hear my speeches, and hearken to all my words. ² Behold, now I have opened my mouth, my tongue hath spoken in my mouth. ³ My words shall be of the uprightness of my heart; and my lips shall utter knowledge clearly. ⁴ The Spirit of God hath made me, and the breath of the Almighty hath given me life. ⁵ If thou canst answer me, set thy words in order before me, stand up. ⁶ Behold, I am according to thy wish in God's stead; I also am formed out of the clay. ⁷ Behold, my terror shall not make thee afraid, neither shall my hand be heavy upon thee.

⁸ 'Surely thou hast spoken in mine hearing, and I have heard the voice of thy words, saying, ⁹ "I am clean without transgression, I am innocent; neither is there iniquity in me." ¹⁰ Behold, he findeth occasions against me, he counteth me

for his enemy, ¹¹he putteth my feet in the stocks, he marketh all my paths.

¹²'Behold, in this thou art not just; I will answer thee, that God is greater than man. ¹³Why dost thou strive against him? For he giveth not account of any of his matters. ¹⁴For God speaketh once, yea twice, yet man perceiveth it not. ¹⁵In a dream, in a vision of the night, when deep sleep falleth upon men, in slumberings upon the bed; ¹⁶then he openeth the ears of men, and sealeth their instruction, ¹⁷that he may withdraw man from his purpose, and hide pride from man. ¹⁸He keepeth back his soul from the pit, and his life from perishing by the sword. ¹⁹He is chastened also with pain upon his bed, and the multitude of his bones with strong pain; ²⁰so that his life abhorreth bread, and his soul dainty meat. ²¹His flesh is consumed away, that it cannot be seen; and his bones that were not seen stick out. ²²Yea, his soul draweth near unto the grave, and his life to the destroyers. ²³If there be a messenger with him, an interpreter, one among a thousand, to shew unto man his uprightness; ²⁴then he is gracious unto him, and saith, "Deliver him from going down to the pit; I have found a ransom. ²⁵His flesh shall be fresher than a child's: he shall return to the days of his youth." ²⁶He shall pray unto God, and he will be favour-able unto him, and he shall see his face with joy; for he will render unto man his righteousness. ²⁷He looketh upon men, and if any say, "I have sinned, and perverted that which was right, and it profited me not;" ²⁸he will deliver his soul from going into the pit, and his life shall see the light.

²⁹'Lo, all these things worketh God oftentimes with man, ³⁰to bring back his soul from the pit, to be enlightened with the light of the living. ³¹Mark well, O Job, hearken unto me: hold thy peace, and I will speak. ³²If thou hast any thing to say, answer me; speak, for I desire to justify thee. ³³If not, hearken unto me: hold thy peace, and I shall teach thee wisdom.'

34

Furthermore Elihu answered and said, ²'Hear my words, O ye wise men; and give ear unto me, ye that have knowledge. ³For the ear trieth words, as the mouth tasteth meat. ⁴Let us choose to us judgment; let us know among ourselves what is good. ⁵For Job hath said, I am righteous; and God hath taken away my judgment. ⁶Should I lie against my right? My wound is incurable without transgression. ⁷What man is like Job, who drinketh up scorning like water, ⁸which goeth in company with the workers of iniquity, and walketh with wicked men? ⁹For he hath said, "It profiteth a man nothing that he should delight himself with God."

¹⁰'Therefore hearken unto me, ye men of understanding: far be it from God, that he should do wickedness; and from the Almighty, that he should commit iniquity. ¹¹For the work of a man shall he render unto him, and cause every man to find according to his ways. ¹²Yea, surely God will not do wickedly, neither will the Almighty pervert judgment. ¹³Who hath given him a charge over the earth? Or who hath disposed the whole world? ¹⁴If he set his heart upon man, if he gather unto himself his spirit and his breath, ¹⁵all flesh shall perish together, and man shall turn again unto dust.

¹⁶ 'If now thou hast understanding, hear this: hearken to the voice of my words. ¹⁷ Shall even he that hateth right govern? And wilt thou condemn him that is most just? ¹⁸ Is it fit to say to a king, "Thou art wicked?" and to princes, "Ye are ungodly"? ¹⁹ How much less to him that accepteth not the persons of princes, nor regardeth the rich more than the poor? For they all are the work of his hands. ²⁰ In a moment shall they die, and the people shall be troubled at midnight, and pass away; and the mighty shall be taken away without hand.

²¹ 'For his eyes are upon the ways of man, and he seeth all his goings. ²² There is no darkness, nor shadow of death, where the workers of iniquity may hide themselves. ²³ For he will not lay upon man more than right; that he should enter into judgment with God. ²⁴ He shall break in pieces mighty men without number, and set others in their stead. ²⁵ Therefore he knoweth their works, and he overturneth them in the night, so that they are destroyed. ²⁶ He striketh them as wicked men in the open sight of others, ²⁷ because they turned back from him, and would not consider any of his ways, ²⁸ so that they cause the cry of the poor to come unto him, and he heareth the cry of the afflicted. ²⁹ When he giveth quietness, who then can make trouble? And when he hideth his face, who then can behold him? Whether it be done against a nation, or against a man only: ³⁰ that the hypocrite reign not, lest the people be ensnared.

³¹ 'Surely it is meet to be said unto God, "I have borne chastisement, I will not offend any more; ³² that which I see not teach thou me. If I have done iniquity, I will do no more."

³³ Should it be according to thy mind? He will recompense it, whether thou refuse, or whether thou choose; and not I. Therefore speak what thou knowest. ³⁴ Let men of understanding tell me, and let a wise man hearken unto me. ³⁵ Job hath spoken without knowledge, and his words were without wisdom. ³⁶ My desire is that Job may be tried unto the end because of his answers for wicked men. ³⁷ For he addeth rebellion unto his sin, he clappeth his hands among us, and multiplieth his words against God.'

35 Elihu spake moreover, and said, ² 'Thinkest thou this to be right, that thou saidst, "My righteousness is more than God's"? ³ For thou saidst, "What advantage will it be unto thee?" and "What profit shall I have, if I be cleansed from my sin?" ⁴ I will answer thee, and thy companions with thee. ⁵ Look unto the heavens, and see; and behold the clouds which are higher than thou. ⁶ If thou sinnest, what doest thou against him? Or if thy transgressions be multiplied, what doest thou unto him? ⁷ If thou be righteous, what givest thou him? Or what receiveth he of thine hand? ⁸ Thy wickedness may hurt a man as thou art; and thy righteousness may profit the son of man.

⁹ 'By reason of the multitude of oppressions they make the oppressed to cry; they cry out by reason of the arm of the mighty. ¹⁰ But none saith, "Where is God my maker, who giveth songs in the night; ¹¹ who teacheth us more than the beasts of the earth, and maketh us wiser than the fowls of heaven?" ¹² There they cry, but none giveth answer, because

of the pride of evil men. ¹³ Surely God will not hear vanity, neither will the Almighty regard it. ¹⁴ Although thou sayest thou shalt not see him, yet judgment is before him; therefore trust thou in him. ¹⁵ But now, because it is not so, he hath visited in his anger; yet he knoweth it not in great extremity. ¹⁶ Therefore doth Job open his mouth in vain; he multiplieth words without knowledge.'

36 Elihu also proceeded, and said, ² 'Suffer me a little, and I will shew thee that I have yet to speak on God's behalf. ³ I will fetch my knowledge from afar, and will ascribe righteousness to my Maker. ⁴ For truly my words shall not be false; he that is perfect in knowledge is with thee.

⁵ 'Behold, God is mighty, and despiseth not any; he is mighty in strength and wisdom. ⁶ He preserveth not the life of the wicked, but giveth right to the poor. ⁷ He withdraweth not his eyes from the righteous; but with kings are they on the throne; yea, he doth establish them for ever, and they are exalted. ⁸ And if they be bound in fetters, and be holden in cords of affliction; ⁹ then he sheweth them their work, and their transgressions that they have exceeded. ¹⁰ He openeth also their ear to discipline, and commandeth that they return from iniquity. ¹¹ If they obey and serve him, they shall spend their days in prosperity, and their years in pleasures. ¹² But if they obey not, they shall perish by the sword, and they shall die without knowledge. ¹³ 'But the hypocrites in heart heap up wrath: they cry not when he bindeth them. ¹⁴ They die in youth, and their life is among the unclean. ¹⁵ He delivereth

the poor in his affliction, and openeth their ears in oppression. ¹⁶ Even so would he have removed thee out of the strait into a broad place, where there is no straitness; and that which should be set on thy table should be full of fatness.

¹⁷ 'But thou hast fulfilled the judgment of the wicked; judgment and justice take hold on thee. ¹⁸ Because there is wrath, beware lest he take thee away with his stroke; then a great ransom cannot deliver thee. ¹⁹ Will he esteem thy riches? No, not gold, nor all the forces of strength. ²⁰ Desire not the night, when people are cut off in their place. ²¹ Take heed, regard not iniquity; for this hast thou chosen rather than affliction. ²² Behold, God exalteth by his power; who teacheth like him? ²³ Who hath enjoined him his way? Or who can say, "Thou hast wrought iniquity"?

²⁴ 'Remember that thou magnify his work, which men behold. ²⁵ Every man may see it; man may behold it afar off. ²⁶ Behold, God is great, and we know him not, neither can the number of his years be searched out. ²⁷ For he maketh small the drops of water; they pour down rain according to the vapour thereof, ²⁸ which the clouds do drop and distil upon man abundantly. ²⁹ Also can any understand the spreadings of the clouds, or the noise of his tabernacle? ³⁰ Behold, he spreadeth his light upon it, and covereth the bottom of the sea. ³¹ For by them judgeth he the people; he giveth meat in abundance. ³² With clouds he covereth the light; and commandeth it not to shine by the cloud that cometh betwixt. ³³ The noise thereof sheweth concerning it, the cattle also concerning the vapour.

37 'At this also my heart trembleth, and is moved out of his place. ² Hear attentively the noise of his voice, and the sound that goeth out of his mouth. ³ He directeth it under the whole heaven, and his lightning unto the ends of the earth. ⁴ After it a voice roareth; he thundereth with the voice of his excellency; and he will not stay them when his voice is heard. ⁵ God thundereth marvellously with his voice; great things doeth he, which we cannot comprehend. ⁶ For he saith to the snow, "Be thou on the earth;" likewise to the small rain, and to the great rain of his strength. ' He sealeth up the hand of every man; that all men may know his work. ⁸ Then the beasts go into dens, and remain in their places. ⁹ Out of the south cometh the whirlwind; and cold out of the north. ¹⁰ By the breath of God frost is given; and the breadth of the waters is straitened. ¹¹ Also by watering he wearieth the thick cloud, he scattereth his bright cloud; ¹² and it is turned round about by his counsels, that they may do whatsoever he commandeth them upon the face of the world in the earth. ¹³ He causeth it to come, whether for correction, or for his land, or for mercy.

¹⁴ 'Hearken unto this, O Job: stand still, and consider the wondrous works of God. ¹⁵ Dost thou know when God disposed them, and caused the light of his cloud to shine? ¹⁶ Dost thou know the balancings of the clouds, the wondrous works of him which is perfect in knowledge? ¹⁷ How thy garments are warm, when he quieteth the earth by the south wind? ¹⁸ Hast thou with him spread out the sky, which is strong, and as a molten looking glass? ¹⁹ Teach us what we shall say

unto him; for we cannot order our speech by reason of darkness. ²⁰ Shall it be told him that I speak? If a man speak, surely he shall be swallowed up. ²¹And now men see not the bright light which is in the clouds; but the wind passeth, and cleanseth them. ²² Fair weather cometh out of the north; with God is terrible majesty. ²³ Touching the Almighty, we cannot find him out; he is excellent in power, and in judg-ment, and in plenty of justice; he will not afflict. ²⁴ Men do therefore fear him; he respecteth not any that are wise of heart.'

38

Then the Lord answered Job out of the whirlwind, and said,

²'Who is this that darkeneth counsel by words
without knowledge?
³ Gird up now thy loins like a man;
for I will demand of thee, and answer thou me.
⁴ Where wast thou when I laid
the foundations of the earth?
Declare, if thou hast understanding.
⁵ Who hath laid the measures thereof,
if thou knowest?
Or who hath stretched the line upon it?
⁶ Whereupon are the foundations thereof fastened?
Or who laid the corner stone thereof,
⁷ when the morning stars sang together,
and all the sons of God shouted for joy?
⁸ Or who shut up the sea with doors,

when it brake forth,
    as if it had issued out of the womb,
⁹ when I made the cloud the garment thereof,
    and thick darkness a swaddling-band for it,
¹⁰ and brake up for it my decreed place,
    and set bars and doors,
¹¹ and said, "Hitherto shalt thou come, but no further:
    and here shall thy proud waves be stayed"?
¹² Hast thou commanded the morning since thy days,
    and caused the dayspring to know his place;
¹³ that it might take hold of the ends of the earth,
    that the wicked might be shaken out of it?
¹⁴ It is turned as clay to the seal;
    and they stand as a garment.
¹⁵ And from the wicked their light is withholden,
    and the high arm shall be broken.
¹⁶ Hast thou entered into the springs of the sea?
    Or hast thou walked in the search of the depth?
¹⁷ Have the gates of death been opened unto thee?
    Or hast thou seen the doors of
        the shadow of death?
¹⁸ Hast thou perceived the breadth of the earth?
    Declare if thou knowest it all.
¹⁹ Where is the way where light dwelleth?
    And as for darkness, where is the place thereof,
²⁰ that thou shouldest take it to the bound thereof,
    and that thou shouldest know the paths
        to the house thereof?

²¹ Knowest thou it, because thou wast then born?
　　Or because the number of thy days is great?
²² Hast thou entered into the treasures of the snow?
　　Or hast thou seen the treasures of the hail,
²³ which I have reserved against the time of trouble,
　　against the day of battle and war?
²⁴ By what way is the light parted,
　　which scattereth the east wind upon the earth?
²⁵ Who hath divided a watercourse
　　for the overflowing of waters,
　　　　or a way for the lightning of thunder;
²⁶ to cause it to rain on the earth, where no man is;
　　on the wilderness, wherein there is no man;
²⁷ to satisfy the desolate and waste ground;
　　and to cause the bud of the tender herb
　　　　to spring forth?
²⁸ Hath the rain a father?
　　Or who hath begotten the drops of dew?
²⁹ Out of whose womb came the ice?
　　And the hoary frost of heaven,
　　　　who hath gendered it?
³⁰ The waters are hid as with a stone,
　　and the face of the deep is frozen.
³¹ Canst thou bind the sweet influences of Pleiades,
　　or loose the bands of Orion?
³² Canst thou bring forth Mazzaroth in his season?
　　Or canst thou guide Arcturus with his sons?
³³ Knowest thou the ordinances of heaven?

Canst thou set the dominion thereof in the earth?
³⁴ Canst thou lift up thy voice to the clouds,
that abundance of waters may cover thee?
³⁵ Canst thou send lightnings, that they may go,
and say unto thee, "Here we are"?
³⁶ Who hath put wisdom in the inward parts?
Or who hath given understanding to the heart?
³⁷ Who can number the clouds in wisdom?
Or who can stay the bottles of heaven,
³⁸ when the dust groweth into hardness,
and the clods cleave fast together?
³⁹ Wilt thou hunt the prey for the lion,
or fill the appetite of the young lions,
⁴⁰ when they couch in their dens,
and abide in the covert to lie in wait?
⁴¹ Who provideth for the raven his food
when his young ones cry unto God,
they wander for lack of meat.'

39

'Knowest thou the time when the wild goats of
the rock bring forth?
Or canst thou mark when the hinds do calve?
² Canst thou number the months that they fulfil?
Or knowest thou the time when they bring forth?
³ They bow themselves,
they bring forth their young ones,
they cast out their sorrows.
⁴ Their young ones are in good liking,

they grow up with corn;

they go forth, and return not unto them.

⁵ Who hath sent out the wild ass free?

Or who hath loosed the bands of the wild ass

⁶ whose house I have made the wilderness,

and the barren land his dwellings?

⁷ He scorneth the multitude of the city,

neither regardeth he the crying of the driver.

⁸ The range of the mountains is his pasture,

and he searcheth after every green thing.

⁹ Will the unicorn be willing to serve thee,

or abide by the crib?

¹⁰ Canst thou bind the unicorn

with his band in the furrow?

Or will he harrow the valleys after thee?

¹¹ Wilt thou trust him, because his strength is great?

Or wilt thou leave thy labour to him?

¹² Wilt thou believe him,

that he will bring home thy seed,

and gather it into thy barn?

¹³ Gavest thou the goodly wings unto the peacocks

or wings and feathers unto the ostrich

¹⁴ which leaveth her eggs in the earth,

and warmeth them in dust,

¹⁵ and forgetteth that the foot may crush them,

or that the wild beast may break them?

¹⁶ She is hardened against her young ones,

as though they were not hers;

her labour is in vain without fear,
¹⁷ because God hath deprived her of wisdom,
neither hath he imparted to her understanding.
¹⁸ What time she lifteth up herself on high,
she scorneth the horse and his rider.
¹⁹ Hast thou given the horse strength?
Hast thou clothed his neck with thunder?
²⁰ Canst thou make him afraid as a grasshopper?
The glory of his nostrils is terrible.
²¹ He paweth in the valley,
and rejoiceth in his strength;
he goeth on to meet the armed men.
²² He mocketh at fear, and is not affrighted;
neither turneth he back from the sword.
²³ The quiver rattleth against him,
the glittering spear and the shield.
²⁴ He swalloweth the ground with fierceness and rage;
neither believeth he
that it is the sound of the trumpet.
²⁵ He saith among the trumpets, "Ha, ha;"
and he smelleth the battle afar off,
the thunder of the captains, and the shouting.
²⁶ Doth the hawk fly by thy wisdom,
and stretch her wings toward the south?
²⁷ Doth the eagle mount up at thy command,
and make her nest on high?
²⁸ She dwelleth and abideth on the rock,
upon the crag of the rock, and the strong place.

²⁹ From thence she seeketh the prey,
and her eyes behold afar off.
³⁰ Her young ones also suck up blood;
and where the slain are, there is she.'

40

Moreover the Lord answered Job, and said,

² 'Shall he that contendeth with the Almighty
instruct him?
He that reproveth God, let him answer it.'

³ Then Job answered the Lord, and said,

⁴ 'Behold, I am vile; what shall I answer thee?
I will lay mine hand upon my mouth.
⁵ Once have I spoken, but I will not answer;
yea, twice, but I will proceed no further.'

⁶ Then answered the Lord unto Job out of the whirlwind,
and said,

⁷ 'Gird up thy loins now like a man;
I will demand of thee, and declare thou unto me.
⁸ Wilt thou also disannul my judgment?
Wilt thou condemn me,
that thou mayest be righteous?
⁹ Hast thou an arm like God?
Or canst thou thunder with a voice like him?
¹⁰ Deck thyself now with majesty and excellency;
and array thyself with glory and beauty.

¹¹ Cast abroad the rage of thy wrath:
    and behold every one that is proud,
        and abase him.
¹² Look on every one that is proud,
    and bring him low;
        and tread down the wicked in their place.
¹³ Hide them in the dust together;
    and bind their faces in secret.
¹⁴ Then will I also confess unto thee
    that thine own right hand can save thee.
¹⁵ Behold now behemoth, which I made with thee;
    he eateth grass as an ox.
¹⁶ Lo now, his strength is in his loins,
    and his force is in the navel of his belly.
¹⁷ He moveth his tail like a cedar:
    the sinews of his stones are wrapped together.
¹⁸ His bones are as strong pieces of brass;
    his bones are like bars of iron.
¹⁹ He is the chief of the ways of God;
    he that made him can make his sword
        to approach unto him.
²⁰ Surely the mountains bring him forth food,
    where all the beasts of the field play.
²¹ He lieth under the shady trees,
    in the covert of the reed, and fens.
²² The shady trees cover him with their shadow;
    the willows of the brook compass him about.
²³ Behold, he drinketh up a river, and hasteth not;

he trusteth that he can draw up Jordan
>into his mouth.
²⁴ He taketh it with his eyes;
>his nose pierceth through snares.'

41

'Canst thou draw out leviathan with an hook?
>Or his tongue with a cord which thou lettest down?
² Canst thou put an hook into his nose?
>Or bore his jaw through with a thorn?
³ Will he make many supplications unto thee?
>Will he speak soft words unto thee?
⁴ Will he make a covenant with thee?
>Wilt thou take him for a servant for ever?
⁵ Wilt thou play with him as with a bird?
>Or wilt thou bind him for thy maidens?
⁶ Shall the companions make a banquet of him?
>Shall they part him among the merchants?
⁷ Canst thou fill his skin with barbed irons
>or his head with fish spears?
⁸ Lay thine hand upon him,
>remember the battle, do no more.
⁹ Behold, the hope of him is in vain; shall not one
>be cast down even at the sight of him?
¹⁰ None is so fierce that dare stir him up;
>who then is able to stand before me?
¹¹ Who hath prevented me, that I should repay him?
>Whatsoever is under the whole heaven is mine.
¹² I will not conceal his parts, nor his power,

nor his comely proportion.

¹³ Who can discover the face of his garment?

Or who can come to him with his double bridle?

¹⁴ Who can open the doors of his face?

His teeth are terrible round about.

¹⁵ His scales are his pride, shut up together

as with a close seal.

¹⁶ One is so near to another,

that no air can come between them.

¹⁷ They are joined one to another, they stick together,

that they cannot be sundered.

¹⁸ By his neesings a light doth shine,

and his eyes are like the eyelids of the morning.

¹⁹ Out of his mouth go burning lamps,

and sparks of fire leap out.

²⁰ Out of his nostrils goeth smoke,

as out of a seething pot or caldron.

²¹ His breath kindleth coals,

and a flame goeth out of his mouth.

²² In his neck remaineth strength,

and sorrow is turned into joy before him.

²³ The flakes of his flesh are joined together;

they are firm in themselves;

they cannot be moved.

²⁴ His heart is as firm as a stone;

yea, as hard as a piece of the nether millstone.

²⁵ When he raiseth up himself, the mighty are afraid;

by reason of breakings they purify themselves.

²⁶ The sword of him that layeth at him cannot hold
   the spear, the dart, nor the habergeon.
²⁷ He esteemeth iron as straw,
   and brass as rotten wood.
²⁸ The arrow cannot make him flee;
   slingstones are turned with him into stubble.
²⁹ Darts are counted as stubble;
   he laugheth at the shaking of a spear.
³⁰ Sharp stones are under him;
   he spreadeth sharp pointed things upon the mire.
³¹ He maketh the deep to boil like a pot;
   he maketh the sea like a pot of ointment.
³² He maketh a path to shine after him;
   one would think the deep to be hoary.
³³ Upon earth there is not his like,
   who is made without fear.
³⁴ He beholdeth all high things;
   he is a king over all the children of pride.'

42

Then Job answered the Lord, and said,

² 'I know that thou canst do every thing,
   and that no thought can be withholden from thee.
³ Who is he that hideth counsel without knowledge?
   Therefore have I uttered that I understood not;
      things too wonderful for me,
   which I knew not.
⁴ Hear, I beseech thee, and I will speak;

I will demand of thee, and declare thou unto me.
⁵ I have heard of thee by the hearing of the ear;
   but now mine eye seeth thee.
⁶ Wherefore I abhor myself,
   and repent in dust and ashes.'

⁷And it was so, that after the Lord had spoken these words unto Job, the Lord said to Eliphaz the Temanite, 'My wrath is kindled against thee, and against thy two friends; for ye have not spoken of me the thing that is right, as my servant Job hath. ⁸ Therefore take unto you now seven bullocks and seven rams, and go to my servant Job, and offer up for yourselves a burnt offering; and my servant Job shall pray for you, for him will I accept lest I deal with you after your folly, in that ye have not spoken of me the thing which is right, like my servant Job.' ⁹ So Eliphaz the Temanite and Bildad the Shuhite and Zophar the Naamathite went, and did according as the Lord commanded them; the Lord also accepted Job.

¹⁰And the Lord turned the captivity of Job, when he prayed for his friends; also the Lord gave Job twice as much as he had before. ¹¹ Then came there unto him all his brethren, and all his sisters, and all they that had been of his acquaintance before, and did eat bread with him in his house; and they bemoaned him, and comforted him over all the evil that the Lord had brought upon him; every man also gave him a piece of money, and every one an earring of gold. ¹² So the Lord blessed the latter end of Job more than his beginning; for he had fourteen thousand sheep, and six thousand camels, and a

thousand yoke of oxen, and a thousand she asses. ¹³ He had also seven sons and three daughters. ¹⁴And he called the name of the first Jemima; and the name of the second Kezia; and the name of the third Kerenhappuch. ¹⁵And in all the land were no women found so fair as the daughters of Job; and their father gave them inheritance among their brethren. ¹⁶After this lived Job an hundred and forty years, and saw his sons, and his sons' sons, even four generations. ¹⁷So Job died, being old and full of days.